TRAVELS
WITH A DONKEY
in the Cévennes

Robert Louis Stevenson

Illustrated Edition

TRAVELS WITH A DONKEY
in the Cévennes

Robert Louis Stevenson

Introduction by Robin Neillands

Illustrated Edition

Chatto & Windus London

First published in this edition in 1988 by Chatto & Windus Ltd.,
30 Bedford Square, London WC1B 3RP.

First published in Great Britain in 1879 by Routledge & Kegan
Paul Ltd.

Introduction © 1986 Beanstalk Books Ltd.
This design © 1986 Beanstalk Books Ltd.
This book conceived, edited and designed by Beanstalk Books Ltd.,
89 Park Hill, London SW4 9NX.

Designed by Julian Holland.

Picture research by Anne-Marie Ehrlich.

Printed in Great Britain by William Clowes & Sons Ltd.

Typeset by Chambers Wallace Ltd., London.

British Library Cataloguing in Publication Data

Stevenson, Robert Louis
    Travels with a donkey in the Cévennes.
    1. Cévennes Mountains (France)—
    Description and travel
    I. Title
    914.4′804812   DC611.C424

    ISBN 0-7011-3327-9

Cover design by Cooper Dale
Front cover photograph by James Ravilious
Cover lettering by Toni Rann

Acknowledgements
Abbey of Our Lady of the Snows: 70,74,75,88.
Robin Adshead, photographer: 11,33.
Musées d'Aurillac. Courtesy of Abbé Pierre. René Vallette
paintings used date from 1921-28: 44,48,52,53,77,99,115.
Beinecke Rare Book and Manuscript Library of Yale University:
10,38,39,47.
Bibliotheque Nationale, Paris: 54,67,78,81,89,121.
British Library: 43,61,83,98,102,118,121,125.
Tony Foster, artist: 45 – with thanks to the owners Mr and Mrs
Sandys, 80,97,100 – with thanks to the owners Henderson and
Martine McCartney, 109 – with thanks to the owners Mr and Mrs
Langolands.
French Government Tourist Office: 19.
Albert Kahn Collection, Boulogne, Prefecture des Hauts-de-Seine.
Photographs used date from 1911-16: 41,65,68,73,101,112.
Reunioné des Musées Nationaux: Saint-André-en-Morvan: 104.
James Ravilious, photographer: 13,14,17,18,20,25,26,29,31,37,51,
56,59,76,90,94,117.

Contents

Introduction
——Robert Louis Stevenson's Life and Works——

The sudden death of Robert Louis Stevenson in 1894 brought an all too early end to a life of considerable literary distinction. Looking back on Stevenson's achievements, the modern reader remembers him as the author of popular works or children's tales. This was not how Stevenson's work was viewed during his lifetime or in the decades immediately after his death. He was a lion to his colleagues and contemporaries, and when the news of his death arrived from Samoa, it brought with it a deep sense of loss. 'Stevenson is dead,' wrote Arthur Quiller-Couch, 'and now there is nobody left to write for. Our children and grandchildren shall rejoice in his books, but we of the living generation, possessed in the living man something they will not know. So long as he lived, though it were far from us – though we had never spoken to him and he perhaps had barely heard our names – we always wrote our best for Stevenson.'

Robert Louis Stevenson, 1850-94. Painting by Sir William Blake Richmond, 1887.

Stevenson's books have not only given pleasure to later generations, they have also made an effortless transformation into new areas of an expanding media, into radio, into films, into television serials, endlessly remade, constantly retold.

There can be no finer epitaph for a writer than the unstinting admiration and affection of his contemporaries, and their praise too, has stood the test of time. Few today would deny that the author of *Treasure Island, Kidnapped, The Black Arrow, Dr Jekyll and Mr Hyde, The Master of Ballantrae, Catriona, Weir of Hermiston,* and *A Child's Garden of Verses,* all still in print a hundred years after his death, must have been an author of genius, though Stevenson himself laid no claim to that title. He thought of himself simply as a teller of tales, and to that list of tales one should certainly add *Travels with a Donkey in the Cévennes,* his first successful book and one that is still regarded as a must for every traveller's library.

*   *   *

Robert Louis Balfour Stevenson was born in Edinburgh on 13th November 1850, the only child of Thomas Stevenson and his wife Margaret, and grandson of Robert Stevenson, civil engineer. In the previous century, the Stevenson family were merchants, trading to the West Indies, but for the last three generations they had been consultant engineers and architects, acting in that capacity to the marvellously-named 'Board of Northern Lights'.

Robert Stevenson, Louis' grandfather, became chief consulting engineer to the Board of Northern Lights in 1807, and immediately undertook the construction of the Bell Rock lighthouse, a formidable task in the face of great natural difficulties, which took four years to

complete and excited the attention and admiration of the entire nation. His son, Thomas, followed his father into the business and made his name with the building of the Skerryvore light, and by the time Louis was born, the family reputation was well established. They were consulting engineers to the New Zealand, Indian and Japanese Board of Lights and, as well as acting in their engineering capacity, the Stevensons were Inspectors of Lighthouses in Scotland. Young Louis frequently accompanied his father on his tours of inspection and they once visited no less than seventeen lighthouses in a single day, a considerable feat for a boy who never enjoyed the best of health.

Young Louis – he was never called Robert and changed his second name from Lewis to Louis when he was about eighteen and living in France – was a sickly child, with a chronic bronchial condition, and the family hoped that these open-air excursions would do him good, but his health remained unstable and in 1864 he made his first visit to France and spent the winter with his mother in Menton. These early years may provide some clue to Stevenson's development as a writer; an only child, ill and away from school, unable to join other children in games, will often devote himself to reading and the exercise of the imagination, but whenever he was well enough to do so, young Stevenson continued to travel. Apart from tours about Scotland with his father, he went to Germany and Holland in 1862, to Italy in 1863, and after returning from France in the spring of 1863, spent the next two winters in Torquay. The family were well-to-do, and could afford private tutors, though Stevenson himself said later, when speaking of this time, that 'Throughout my boyhood and youth I was known and pointed out as an idler, and yet I was always busy on my private end, which was to learn to write.'

His family had decided that he too should follow in his father's footsteps, and in 1867 he entered Edinburgh University as an engineering student, but he had little interest in the profession and was a notable absentee from lectures, and from the tutorials offered by Flemming Jenkin, the Professor of Engineering, although the Professor and his reluctant student soon became close friends. His vacations were still spent visiting the various works then under construction by his father's firm, but by the time Stevenson was nineteen, the family were forced to admit that their son cared for nothing but literature. This was a considerable blow to his father, who declared that writing was no profession to follow and suggested that Louis might study instead for the Bar. At the age of twenty-one Louis began his legal studies and was called to the Bar in July 1875, when he was twenty-five years old.

Stevenson had been writing, with little success, since the age of sixteen, but during his studies for the Bar he had become acquainted

James Ravilious, the photographer, followed Stevenson's route. A scene on the road above La Vernède.

with Sidney Colvin, then Slade Professor of Fine Arts, a Fellow of Trinity College, Cambridge, and later on Keeper of Prints at the British Museum. Colvin encouraged Stevenson and in 1873 sent one of his essays, called 'Roads' to the *Portfolio* magazine, which published and paid for it, the first money Stevenson had ever received for his writing. Stevenson's health continued to be a problem during his student years, and he spent most of the winters in Menton, joined often by Sidney Colvin and his wife, developing a love of warm climates and a good command of the French language.

By 1875 Stevenson's student years were clearly over, but it was equally obvious that the law held as little appeal for him as had engineering; Stevenson simply wanted to write. This provoked a breach with his father, who nevertheless granted his son an allowance of £80 a year, and with this and such sums as he could earn by articles and book reviews, Stevenson survived and was happy. He managed to spend an increasing amount of time in France, either visiting the Latin Quarter of Paris, or at Barbizon, in the Forest of Fontainebleau, two miles outside the city, which was then a popular centre for writers and painters, notably those of the early Impressionist school.

From here, in 1876, he made a canoe trip along the rivers and canals of France and Belgium, from the city of Antwerp south to Pontoise. He was accompanied on this journey by Sir Walter Simpson, a close friend, and their travels were not without incident, for at one point Stevenson was briefly arrested as a spy. This brought their voyage to an abrupt end, although Stevenson managed to complete a book about it. *An Inland Voyage*, which was his first full-length work, was published in 1873.

When the travellers returned to Barbizon, they found the artistic community in turmoil. Before their departure, only three weeks previously, this had been largely a masculine society, though alleviated by the regular arrival of models and lady friends from Paris. Now an American lady had arrived, a Mrs Fanny Osborne, who was estranged from her husband, accompanied by two children, and declaring herself to be an artist. She was ten years older than Stevenson. In the small artistic world around Grez and Barbizon they soon met, and as quickly fell in love. In 1879 he followed her back to America, and in 1880, when Stevenson was thirty-one, they were married.

In the interval he travelled south to the wild country of the Auvergne and at the end of September 1878 he left the little town of Le Monastier in the Vélay, accompanied by '. . . a diminutive she-ass, not much bigger than a dog, the colour of a mouse'. This was Modestine, his donkey, and the story of their travels provided the theme for his first notable book.

*　　*　　*

Le Monastier, where the walk begins. Stevenson describes it as being situated in 'a pleasant highland valley'.

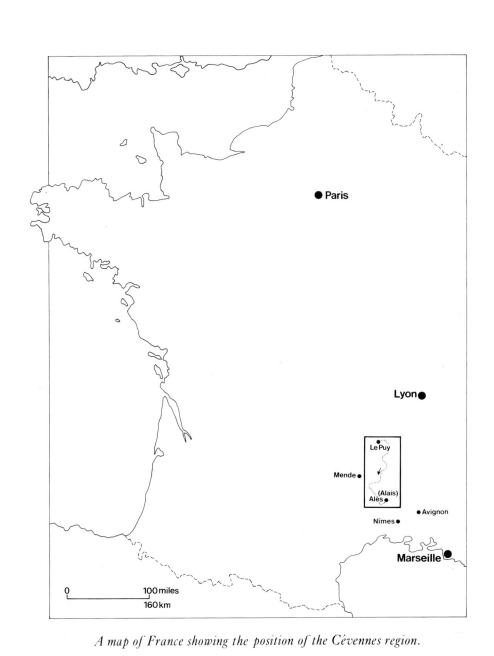

A map of France showing the position of the Cévennes region.

In *Travels with a Donkey,* Stevenson gives no hint of the reasons which motivated him to undertake the journey. Perhaps it was to take a break from the close society of Barbizon, perhaps it was to recover from the sudden absence of Mrs Osborne, who had returned to the United States in an effort to obtain her divorce, perhaps it was simply to get away and think, and perhaps it was just to travel. In this book, Stevenson provides all true travellers with that most quotable quote, 'For my part, I travel not to go anywhere, but to go. I travel for travel's sake. The great affair is to move.'

Stevenson's choice of equipment was, to say the least, eccentric. He decided to do without a tent and settled instead for a sleeping sack into which he stowed some books, a leg of cold mutton, a bottle of Beaujolais, an egg-beater, and a considerable quantity of black and white bread. The size and weight of his supplies called for a beast of burden, and for this he purchased Modestine for sixty-five francs and a glass of brandy. Stevenson had no idea how to load or drive a donkey, and for the first few days treated his small companion abominably, beating her constantly or urging her on with a goad. Only as their journey continued did his skill develop and his affection for her grow.

As journeys go, Stevenson's trip with Modestine covers no great distance, a mere one hundred and twenty miles across the hills and river valleys to the town of St-Jean-du-Gard in the heart of the

Cévennes. In his book Stevenson claims that 'taken largely' his entire journey falls within the Cévennes, but this is not really so. He begins in the Vélay, that rich, green, and once volcanic country that lies about the pilgrim city of Le Puy in the Auvergne, close to the extinct cone of Mont Mézenc, and not far from the Gerbier de Jonc where the river Loire rises, although that great river is already a considerable stream before Stevenson crossed it at Goudet on the first day of his travels.

From here the journey skirted the western edge of the ancient Viverais, now the Ardèche, and passed on south into the Gévaudan, a wild country still remote, off any other notable tourist route and once the haunt of the fabulous Bête du Gévaudan, a great wolf, some say a werewolf, which preyed on the local people and their flocks until the King himself sent a huntsman from Paris, who dispatched it with a silver bullet. Perhaps this is why Stevenson included a revolver among his list of stores; there were certainly wolves in the hills hereabouts when Stevenson passed this way, whatever the truth of the legend.

Once well into the Gévaudan, Stevenson turned off the direct route south, and spent several days in the Trappist monastery of Notre-Dame-des-Neiges, Our Lady of the Snows, which lies tucked into a small valley, a mile or so east of the little village of La Bastide Puylaurens. This monastery still stands, and the monks are still willing to welcome those walkers who follow in Stevenson's footsteps,

A peaceful scene at La Vernède photographed by James Ravilious.

Stevenson called his walk 'an up-and-down journey'.

offering rooms in their guesthouse, or shelter in one of their barns.

After Notre-Dame-des-Neiges, Stevenson and his donkey journeyed west, along the rushing little torrent of the Chassezac, and at Chasserades turned south into the first of the mountains which lay across his path and barred the route to the Cévennes. From this point on it was an up-and-down journey, for Stevenson seems to have headed directly for the summit of every hill, climbing first over the Mont de Goulet at 1497 metres, down into the valley by Le Bleymard, then up again over the 1699 metre peak of Mont Lozère, from which

one can hope to see the distant blue streak of the Mediterranean many miles to the south.

Here, south of Mont Lozère, the Cévennes really begin. The Cévennes is a rugged range of hills and mountains, an outcrop running out south and west from the Massif Central, cloaked with dwarf oak and juniper, seamed by the many rushing tributaries of the river Gardon. It is still a remote and virtually uninhabited place, dotted with long-abandoned farms and hamlets, and was once the country of the Camisards, those Protestants who, uniformed only in their shirts, fought the Royal Army, in a long and bitter rebellion.

As soon as Henry of Navarre ascended the throne of France as Henri IV in 1589, he issued the Edict of Nantes, granting religious

Florac, described by Stevenson as having 'an old castle, an alley of planes, many quaint street-corners, and a live fountain welling from the hill'.

toleration to his Protestant subjects, who had been his chief supporters during the Wars of Religion. His policy of toleration was not followed by his successors, and in 1685 Louis XIV revoked the Edict of Nantes, and plunged his country into chaos. The most immediate effect of the Revocation was to deny the Protestants – or Huguenots – the right to practise their religion, and many promptly left France for ever. More than 100,000 Huguenots fled across the seas, many of them to England. The Protestants of the Cévennes, the Cévenoles, were made of sterner stuff, and they stayed in their hills and resisted the Royal Edict.

When Stevenson passed this way in 1878, the Camisards' struggle had only just passed out of living memory, for the Camisard rebellion endured until the 1790s, when the Revolutionary Government granted religious toleration to the beleaguered Protestant communities of the Cévennes, who had resisted the assaults of the Catholic King's troops for the best part of a hundred years.

The most popular method used to coerce the local people into the Catholic faith was the *dragonnade,* when troops, usually dragoons, were billeted in the villages and fed, horse and man, at the expense of the residents. The Cévenoles resisted the *dragonnades* and their resistance eventually flared into open revolt. After a Catholic priest was killed in 1702, an all-out civil war raged in the Cévennes for two years, and the revolt sputtered on until 1789 when freedom of worship was re-established.

The Camisard uprising has left an indelible impression on the Cévennes and the local people, which is still noticeable today and must have been even more in evidence a hundred years ago. The population is scanty, the villages small and enclosed by walls, the advertised religion noticeably Protestant. The Cévennes are still very much as Stevenson knew them and these wild, beautiful, and sadly romantic hills have now been declared a National Park, which should preserve their beauty for at least the foreseeable future.

Stevenson passed through the Camisard country, through Florac on the Tarn, up the valley of the little river Mimente, vanishing into the thick woods for a day or so; twelve days after leaving Le Monastier, Stevenson and Modestine arrived at St-Jean-du-Gard and parted for ever. Stevenson sold Modestine, 'saddle and all', for thirty-five francs, and her eventual fate is not recorded.

*　　　*　　　*

In the summer of 1879, Stevenson, who had by then written the story of his travels and returned to Scotland, followed Mrs Osborne to America where, in 1880, they were married. They lived in California, where the mild climate and sunshine benefited Stevenson's lungs which were infected with tuberculosis. With a family to support, Stevenson now began to write in earnest and with increasing success. *Travels with a Donkey in the Cévennes* appeared in 1879, *Treasure*

Island in 1883, *A Child's Garden of Verses* in 1885, *Dr Jekyll and Mr Hyde* and *Kidnapped* in 1886, and *The Master of Ballantrae* in 1889. These books were the high points of his work but in addition he wrote a host of other works, including many essays and articles. His labours were interrupted by bouts of ill health and frequent journeys between America and the warmer parts of Europe, where he returned frequently to rest and regain his strength in Nice or Davos or Bournemouth.

Real health, like real riches, continued to elude him, for although he was able to support his wife and step-children by constant effort, he once wrote to Sidney Colvin that it was not until 1886, when he was thirty-six, that his income first exceeded £300 a year. In that year he published *Dr Jekyll and Mr Hyde*, his second popular success after *Treasure Island*, and the one by which he is perhaps best remembered. *Dr Jekyll and Mr Hyde* made Stevenson famous, and his financial problems became less pressing.

In the spring of 1888, Stevenson's American publisher, who like many of Stevenson's friends was increasingly concerned for his health, offered him the large advance of £2000 to make a cruise of the South Pacific, and write the story of his voyages. Stevenson and his family left San Francisco on the schooner *Casco*, and spent six months cruising in the Society Islands and the Marquesas, before spending another six months in Honolulu. Stevenson wrote about this voyage in *The Wrecker*, and notes in the book that his health had been so much restored by the breezes of the Southern Ocean that '. . . even my bones are sweeter to me'.

In September 1890, having completed *The Master of Ballantrae* during the voyage, Stevenson arrived at Apia, Samoa, where, his health and finances much improved, he purchased an estate of four hundred acres, which he called *Vailima*, and settled down to write the first of his South Pacific tales, *The Bottle Imp*. He was now thirty-nine, and was to spend the rest of his life in the Pacific. In the next four years he wrote, among many other works, *Catriona*, the sequel to *Kidnapped*, a short history of his ancestors, *A Family of Engineers*, and his last book *Weir of Hermiston*, which was still uncompleted at the time of his death. His health began to deteriorate again in January 1893 and his efforts to make the Vailima estate pay its way proved another burden, though one which in no way affected his consistent good humour. He died of apoplexy on 3rd December 1894, and was buried on the summit of Pala Mountain, a thousand feet or more above the sea.

* * *

On 18th December 1894, two weeks after his death, *The Times* published his obituary, devoting a full column to his life and work, and noting that his death '. . . leaves a melancholy blank in the literary world, which no one can ever appreciably fill'. In the years which followed his death, the articles and biographies published by his friends and admirers paid tribute to a man who was both greatly respected as a writer and, a rarer tribute in any walk of life, very much loved for himself. Then, inevitably, reaction set in and for a while Stevenson's work attracted little critical acclaim, although his books continued to be popular with that most important audience, the readers. More recently, the scales have tipped the other way, and Stevenson now fairly commands a respected place in the world of English letters, with his work being constantly reprinted and re-published. Reading his books, and those written about him by his friends, one is left with the impression of a man from whom there was always something to be learned, but also of a man with a warm heart and few pretensions. He was indeed a great writer, but was probably just as happy to be what the Samoans came to call him when he lived among them during the last years of his life – *Tusitala*, a teller of tales.

-*The Robert Louis Stevenson Trail*-

In recent years, a fresh accolade has fallen on the unwitting shoulders of our more popular writers. If their work entertains, creates a sense of place and attracts a wide audience, the country in which it is set may become a tourist attraction. Such is fame in the last quarter of the twentieth century, and so we have the Brontë and the Hardy country or, and of more recent date, the Herriot hills and dales of Yorkshire. Even people who rarely read a book are drawn to these places and like to wander through those parts where the characters they have heard about or seen on the television screen are supposed to have existed. It was this kind of thinking, rather than any idea of a memorial to his walk with Modestine, which led to the creation of the Robert Louis Stevenson Trail in 1978, the centenary year of his travels in the Cévennes.

At the early months of that year, I was approached by the French Government Tourist Office and asked if I could suggest some way of highlighting their promotion theme for 1978, when their efforts were to be concentrated on the *arrière-pays*, the back-country of France, with the aim of attracting tourists to those remote parts of that fascinating country, which were, and still are, ravaged by massive depopulation, as local people abandon the land and seek an easier living in the cities.

At that point however, coincidence took a hand. I had just finished writing an article on the life of Robert Louis Stevenson, and so his walk with Modestine was fresh in my mind. Would it not be an idea, I suggested, in this, the centenary year of his travels, to get a group of writers together and do the walk again? The British have a love of anniversaries and this seemed a unique and enjoyable way to bring a little-known and beautiful part of France to the attention of a wider audience.

The idea was accepted, but it seemed advisable to make a small reconnaissance of the route to see if the walk was still possible, and our visit to France soon revealed that other people were thinking along the same lines. The people of Le Monastier-sur-Gazeille and the Cévennes were themselves preparing to re-open the route under the leadership of various local mayors and a redoubtable Scots lady, Madame Pat Villette, who had married a Frenchman and now lived in Decazeville. She was acting as liaison officer between Stevenson's devotees in Scotland and France, and plans were well advanced. Pots of blue and white paint were being distributed to mark the route, St Andrew's flag was flying everywhere, bunting was being strung across village streets, and cultural groups were planning visits to and fro. Fortunately, no one had yet decided to retrace the walk, so that task at least was still open to us, one which we hastened to fulfil. Five other outdoor journalists were assembled and instructed to get fit, and at the end of September we arrived in Le Monastier, our equipment in rucksacks rather than on a donkey, attended an enjoyable reception hosted by the local people, and set off early on the following morning to inaugurate the route.

*   *   *

Taken all in all, the path that Stevenson followed, across the Ardèche and Gévaudan, south into the Cévennes, is very much as it was, and with the aid of good maps and his own book, still quite easy to follow. The local people are hospitable, especially to walkers, and although we decided to camp, there is an adequate amount of accommodation available for those who prefer to stay in hotels.

Having to lead Modestine, Stevenson was obliged to follow roads and *drailles,* or drovers' tracks, whenever possible. Many of these have now been metalled over and are public highways. This has the advantage that much of the Trail can be followed on bicycles or by car, but on the other hand, hard roads are unkind to feet, especially when the surface has been heated by a blazing sun. Stevenson reports rain and chilly nights on his twelve-day journey, but we had seven days of relentless sunshine and temperatures in the nineties, which felled two members with heat exhaustion and endowed everyone with an excessive number of blisters. Those who decide to follow Stevenson's journey would be well advised to allow two full weeks for the trip, and travel outside the hot months of summer, carrying as little equipment as possible. Our 30lb rucksacks, full of camping gear, only added to our problems.

Goats at La Vernède.

We had originally decided to take a donkey, more for companionship and colour than as a beast of burden, but a small test during the reconnaissance revealed that, like Stevenson's Modestine, modern donkeys have an all-out speed of one mile an hour, and a mind of their own. Stevenson, by his own admission, treated Modestine abominably in order to keep her moving, but having no heart for that, we

decided to go without one. We obtained one to see us off at the start by the Stevenson obelisk outside the post office in Le Monastier, and she posed prettily for photographs, but we left her behind as we struck out west for our first landmark at Goudet.

The first day took us some twenty miles over the rolling country to the village of Le Bouchet-St-Nicolas, through the villages of Costaros and Goudet. Goudet lies on a bend of the Loire, and is still as Stevenson describes it, with a ruined castle on the hill above, and a comfortable lunch available at the Hôtel de la Loire, on the banks of the river. The hotel is still run by the Senac family, descendants of those whom Stevenson met, and the present Monsieur Senac will, if

An old man gathering wood for his fire.

pressed, go upstairs and return with that engraving of Régis Senac, 'Professor of Fencing and Champion of the Two Americas', which Stevenson mentions in his book.

The people of Bouchet St Nicolas, who turned out in force to welcome us, were somewhat concerned when one of our number, overcome by heat exhaustion, fell down, face forward, into the dust of the main street. The inn where Stevenson stayed has long since vanished and Bouchet is probably now smaller than it was in his day, but we were able to pitch our tents in the yard of the old inn, and were royally entertained that evening by the mayor. Those who do not wish to camp can stay in the small hotel at the Lac du Bouchet, which occupies the crater of an extinct volcano, two miles to the north.

The sun continued to punish us next day as we tramped south, following those white and blue St Andrew crosses which waymarked the path to Landos, and so into the mercifully shaded streets of Pradelles, just in time for a long lunch in a restaurant somewhere along the main street, and a cooling dip for our feet in one of the town's many fountains. Pradelles is a pretty little town, and the footpath out leads past the church that still contains the image of Our Lady of Pradelles, 'which does many miracles though she were of wood'. Sitting in the cool of the church, I began to think we would need one, for the heat was still relentless. That day took us on through Langogne to a green camp site by the little village of St-Flour-de-Mercoire, where once again the local people came out to offer chilled wine and sympathy for our already battered feet.

Day three I remember as something of a trial. The countryside here is steep and wooded, and the footpath ran through Cheylard over the hard, sunbaked ruts of foresters' paths, climbing steadily, through woods and occasional open meadows, down to the village of Luc. Early in the evening we came limping up the path to the monastery of Notre-Dame-de-Neiges, where chief among the many attractions of that hospitable place was a long and well-stocked bar. We were offered a good meal, bunk-beds in the barn and refreshing showers, all for a few francs. Visitors to Notre-Dame-de-Neiges are an extra source of income for this monastic community, and should apply on arrival to the *Père Hôtelière*, who will arrange for meals and accommodation, but the bulk of the monastic income comes from supplying wine to the local towns and villages.

*   *   *

After Notre-Dame-de-Neiges, the real hills begin, and the Trail enters the Cévennes at last, leading off gently enough beside the river Allier, then along a metalled road to beyond Chasserades, from where a footpath leads up to the Mont du Goulet. Indeed, it is noticeable how often Stevenson's travels lead him to the highest peak. Certainly, where they bar the path with their lofty tops, his trail leads directly to the summit, probably because when he asked the peasants for directions to his next stop, they simply pointed to the mountain top and said, "It's over there". Whatever the reason, the southern half of the Robert Louis Stevenson Trail offers plenty of uphill walking. In winter this area is thickly blanketed with snow, so small ski-lifts now scar the slopes both here and on the next mountain, Mont Lozère, where the village of Le Bleymard is a busy ski resort in winter. Passing Le Bleymard and heading south to the open breezy top of Mont Lozère, the visitor finally enters the Parc National des Cévennes, and descends into Pont de Montvert, one of the significant places in the Country of the Camisards. The footpath here is much obstructed by fences and barbed wire, so it is best to work a little east along the ridge to the Col de Finiels, and descend into Pont de Montvert by the D20 road. France is laced by an extensive footpath network called the *Grande Randonnée*, but as yet the Stevenson Trail is not part of the G.R. and therefore subject to obstruction.

Pont de Montvert is a pretty place on the river Tarn, but as Stevenson points out, it has bloody memories. In the early days of the Camisard revolt, this was the headquarters of François de Chayla, Inspector of Catholic Mission, Archpriest of the Cévennes, and a latter-day Torquemada. De Chayla spared no efforts or methods to ensure the locals' conversion to Catholicism, including *dragonnades* and torture, until, one night in 1702, the locals rose against him, broke into his house, dragged him into the main square and cut him to pieces. The death of de Chayla set the Cévennes alight and the two years of open war which followed, between the King's Army and the Cévenoles, were marked with unparalleled atrocities. Captured Cévenoles were shot at once or sent to row out their lives in the galleys, while the women and children were taken away and imprisoned in the fortress of Aigues-Mortes. The Cévenoles still recall the fate of one little girl, Marie Durand, who was imprisoned in the Tour de Constance in Aigues-Mortes at the age of eight and kept there for forty years!

These are sad stories and they must not detract from the present attractions of Pont de Montvert, which is a place to linger in for those who have the time. From here the Trail follows the river west, to Florac, and the road was new, '. . . a smooth sandy ledge', in 1878. Today it is a busy, metalled highway, running in and out of tunnels and no safe place for walking, so wise walkers will cross the river and follow the crest of the hill opposite down to Florac, a fine old town which lies at the top of the beautiful and famous Gorges du Tarn. Florac is a busy place, popular with tourists and full of fine hotels, but we found space on a camp site by the river, and rested here in the shade, getting ready for the next stage of our journey up the valley of the Mimente.

Stevenson went up the Mimente, into the heart of the Cévennes, by following paths which later became the track of the railway. The railway line has long since been grubbed up, but searching in the bushes on the far side of the road we soon found what appeared to be

Pont de Montvert. 'The place with its houses, its lanes, its glaring river-bed, wore an indescribable air of the South.'

an embankment, and a little scuffing about with the heels of our boots turned up the rotting wood of old railway sleepers. With the old route re-established, we decided to follow it, not least because it offered easy, level walking.

This route along the old railway line up the Mimente is both fascinating and spectacular, through long, dark and dripping tunnels, over bridges which creaked alarmingly under our weight, so that we spaced ourselves out and crossed over singly, stepping gingerly from sleeper to sleeper. Those who elect to follow the line today should be even more cautious, or they can follow the minor road that leads up the valley to St-Julian-d'Arpaon, where a friendly *restaurateur* let us camp in his field. He was amply repaid by the vast meal we enjoyed in his restaurant later that evening.

From here, the Trail and the railway line were less easy to follow, and the waymarks, which were always intermittent and not always accurate, now vanished altogether, leaving us to rely completely on Stevenson's book and our maps. These brought us eventually to a clearing in the woods, once the site of a signal box, where the path turned away from the railway and climbed, up and up, ever higher and hotter, out of the woods onto the bare tops where a forest fire had blasted the trees away, and then down the blackened hillside to the *gîte d'étape* at La Serre de La Can, near the village of St. Germain de Calberte.

Gîtes d'étape are common along the *Grande Randonnee* footpaths of France, and are best imagined as unmanned youth hostels, open to walkers, cyclists and pony-trekkers for a few francs a night. They can range in size and comfort from small stone-built huts to fully-furnished, comfortable apartments, and this one at La Serre de La Can fell into the latter category and was supremely comfortable. The *gîte* was established in lofts over the stables in a stud for Arab horses, so we also had delightful little foals scampering about in the paddocks just below. After six days on the Trail we were not a pretty sight, but the *guardian* was kindness itself, showing us to comfortable rooms, turning on the showers and pointing out the shortest path to bar and restaurant. Dinner at La Serre de La Can went on for hours and remains in my memory as one of the high points in a memorable trip.

Next day we decided to linger. That is often the way on a walk; at the start there is the urge to get on and cover the distance, then suddenly the end of the path grows closer, and no one wants the walk to end. We started late, ambling slowly down the hillside to St. Germain de Calberte, giving up another hour there to coffee on a café terrace shaded by vines, and then wandered gently down the road to our last camp site by the bridge at St Etienne-Vallée-Française, on the River Gardon. We pitched our tents along the banks here, just after noon, and spent the afternoon lazing about or floating gently in the river, the perfect way to pass a little time in the green and golden country of the Cévennes.

On our final day we were up early, striking camp swiftly, and getting rapidly underway, fit enough now to ignore the heat of the sun, the weight of our packs and the pain in our feet, following Stevenson's route again, over yet another hill and then, early in the afternoon, down another dusty rutted track onto the main road. One hundred years to the day after Stevenson arrived with Modestine, we walked into the little town of St-Jean-du-Gard and the end of our journey, as well content as Stevenson was with our travels, even *sans* donkey, through the beautiful hills of the Cévennes.

Points of Interest Between the Vélay and the Cévennes

A man working in his garden at St. Germain de Calberte.

Stevenson and Modestine took twelve days to cover the one hundred and twenty miles that lie between Le Monastier-sur-Gazeille and St-Jean-du-Gard, and wise walkers today would probably take the same time, or if possible, a little longer, for there are plenty of points of interest along the way and a number of places where the beauty of the landscape or the charm of a village will make any sensible traveller wish to linger. It is certainly not an area to rush through, but one which amply repays those who like to take their time and wander off the beaten track.

Those who are less energetic may want to retrace the main points of Stevenson's journey by car, and this too is perfectly possible, for only in a few places, say between St-Julian-d'Arpaon and St Germain de Calberte is the route totally impassable to all but walkers. It would be feasible to drive the total distance of Stevenson's journey in well under a day, but those who wish to spend a holiday touring by car from the Vélay to St-Jean-du-Gard in the Cévennes will find plenty of places of interest just on or off the Trail, and all of them are well worth a visit.

The Vélay

Le Monastier lies about fifteen miles south of the city of Le Puy, a fascinating town on the Loire, capital of the volcanic country of the Vélay. The site of Le Puy is remarkable, and noted for the several sharp hills or 'puys' which dominate the city. One of these is crowned by a minute medieval pilgrim chapel, St Michel d'Aiguilhe, reached up a flight of 268 steps, and another, the Rocher Corneille, by a huge (and very ugly) statue of Notre Dame de France, erected in 1860 and forged from the metal of 213 bronze cannons captured from the Russian Army at Sebastapol during the Crimean War. Le Puy is one of the four starting places in France for the Pilgrimage to the Shrine of St James at Santiago de Compostela in Spain, and the cathedral here contains another object of pilgrim veneration, the statue of Our Lady of Le Puy, one of the rare Black Virgins of the Auvergne. Close to Le Puy, but a little to the north, the great castle of Polignac stands on a rocky plateau and is just one of several fortresses that guard the routes into this historic town.

Ardèche and Gévaudan

From Le Monastier, the traveller would be well advised to take a day off the Trail and travel east, into the beautiful country of the Ardèche, through the ski resort and walking centre of Les Estables to two beautiful mountains, Mont Mézenc (1753m) and the cone of the Gerbier de Jonc, worth visiting for themselves and for the views they offer over lovely country which lies all about. A little closer to Le

Monastier lies the ruined castle of Arlempedes, on an escarpment overlooking the Loire, a wonderful spot, especially early in the evening when the sun is going down over the hills.

Following Stevenson's trail to the south, it is the scenery which draws the eye, for this is not a major tourist area, and there are no popular, overcrowded attractions. For all that, this is a beautiful country, a place where all the travellers' clichés come true. Here there really are flower-filled meadows, white with daffodil and wild narcissii in the early days of spring. Here, yoked cattle or oxen still pull the plough. Here you may still see a shepherdess sitting on a rock and playing a pipe to her attentive sheep. A little east of La Bastide Puylaurens, a modern road, the Corniche du Viverais, provides the perfect motoring route into a wildly attractive mountain area.

There is no lack of accommodation, even here, often in small Logis de France hotels, and no visitor on the Stevenson Trail could possibly pass this way without spending at least one night at the monastery of Notre-Dame-des-Neiges, and climbing to the top of the Goudet or Mont Lozère for spectacular views across the Cévennes towards the distant blue of the Mediterranean.

The Tarn and Cévennes

Florac is a pretty place, full of hotels, and a good touring centre for exploring the magnificent Gorges of the Tarn which lie to the north and west, and can be easily followed along the river to Le Rozier, past such charming little places as Ispagnac, Ste-Enimie, to the wonderful Château de la Caze, a medieval fortress which is now a fine hotel, and so up to the viewpoint at the Point Sublime. More intrepid travellers can leave their cars at La Malène and descend the narrows of Les Detroits by canoe. From Le Rozier it is possible to return to Florac across the high open plateau of the Causse Méjean, and rejoin the Robert Louis Stevenson Trail by taking the road from Florac, up the valley of the Mimente and so directly into the Cévennes at the Col de Jalcreste. The National Park of the Cévennes covers a wide area, running south from Mont Lozère to the 1565m peak of Mont Aigoual, a region of rich woodland, open meadow, stone walls, small busy rivers and empty roads, a paradise for lovers of the outdoors.

An ideal way for the motorist to see the best of the Cévennes is to descend first to St Jean du Gard and head up into the Park from there along the high open road that follows the Corniche des Cévennes. This was built by Louis XIV's military engineers to enable the Royal Army's artillery to get into the hills, a great feat of military engineering then and a spectacular journey today, with vast views in all directions.

The farmhouse at Le Mas Soubeyran, near St Jean du Gard, is now a museum to the Camisards. During the revolt this was the head-quarters of one of the Cévenole leaders, Roland, who was captured and executed in 1704. The museum records the struggles and successes of the Camisards, and in particular the fate of those thousands who were taken from their villages and sent to die in the galleys. Further south, between the Cévennes and the sea, the traveller can visit the university town of Montpellier or the fortress city of Aigues-Mortes, the port built by St Louis for the Seventh Crusade and once a prison for the Camisards. I suspect that these last places, attractive and historic as they are, will prove far too crowded and noisy for visitors who have travelled south along the axis of the Robert Louis Stevenson Trail, and passed their days gently and slowly in getting from the far green country of the Vélay to the quiet and empty hills of the southern Cévennes.

Robin Neillands

The village of Luc as seen by Robin Neilland's party. Stevenson found it less congenial and thought it 'an unsightly prospect'.

33

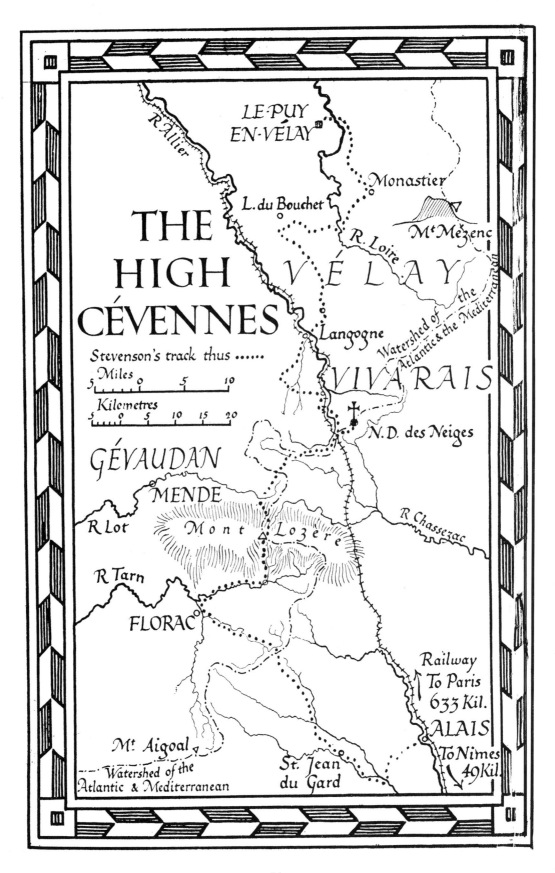

THE HIGH CÉVENNES

Stevenson's track thus ......

Miles

Kilometres

R. Allier

LE·PUY EN·VÉLAY

L. du Bouchet

Monastier

Mt Mézenc

R. Loire

VÉLAY

Langogne

Watershed of the Atlantic & the Mediterranean

VIVARAIS

N.D. des Neiges

GÉVAUDAN

MENDE

R. Lot

Mont Lozère

R. Chassezac

R. Tarn

FLORAC

Railway To Paris 633 Kil.

ALAIS

Mt Aigoal

To Nimes 49 Kil.

Watershed of the Atlantic & Mediterranean

St. Jean du Gard

My Dear Sidney Colvin,

The journey which this little book is to describe was very agreeable and fortunate for me. After an uncouth beginning, I had the best of luck to the end. But we are all travellers in what John Bunyan calls the wilderness of this world – all, too, travellers with a donkey: and the best that we find in our travels is an honest friend. He is a fortunate voyager who finds many. We travel, indeed, to find them. They are the end and the reward of life. They keep us worthy of ourselves; and when we are alone, we are only nearer to the absent.

Every book is, in an intimate sense, a circular letter to the friends of him who writes it. They alone take his meaning; they find private messages, assurances of love, and expressions of gratitude, dropped for them in every corner. The public is but a generous patron who defrays the postage. Yet though the letter is directed to all, we have an old and kindly custom of addressing it on the outside to one. Of what shall a man be proud, if he is not proud of his friends? And so, my dear Sidney Colvin, it is with pride that I sign myself affectionately yours,

R. L. S.

Vélay

Many are the mighty things, and nought is more mighty than man.
. . . He masters by his devices the tenant of the fields.
SOPHOCLES

Who hath loosed the bands of the wild ass?
JOB

The Donkey, the Pack, and the Pack-saddle

IN a little place called Le Monastier, in a pleasant highland valley fifteen miles from Le Puy, I spent about a month of fine days. Monastier is notable for the making of lace, for drunkenness, for freedom of language, and for unparalleled political dissension. There are adherents of each of the four French parties – Legitimists, Orleanists, Imperialists, and Republicans – in this little mountain-town; and they all hate, loathe, decry, and calumniate each other. Except for business purposes, or to give each other the lie in a tavern brawl, they have laid aside even the civility of speech. 'Tis a mere mountain Poland. In the midst of this Babylon I found myself a rallying point; everyone was anxious to be kind and helpful to the stranger. This was not merely from the natural hospitality of mountain people, nor even from the surprise with which I was regarded as a man living of his own free will in Le Monastier, when he might just as well have lived anywhere else in this big world; it arose a good deal from my projected excursion southward through the Cévennes. A traveller of my sort was a thing hitherto unheard of in that district.

A view of the country side around Le Monastier.

Stevenson made twenty-six pencil drawings of the area around Le Monastier. This is an unidentified sketch of a peasant at Vélay.

I was looked upon with contempt, like a man who should project a journey to the moon, but yet with a respectful interest, like one setting forth for the inclement Pole. All were ready to help in my preparations; a crowd of sympathisers supported me at the critical moment of a bargain; not a step was taken but was heralded by glasses round and celebrated by a dinner or a breakfast.

It was already hard upon October before I was ready to set forth, and at the high altitudes over which my road lay there was no Indian summer to be looked for. I was determined, if not to camp out, at least to have the means of camping out in my possession; for there is nothing more harassing to an easy mind than the necessity of reaching shelter by dusk, and the hospitality of a village inn is not always to be reckoned sure by those who trudge on foot. A tent, above all for a solitary traveller, is troublesome to pitch, and troublesome to strike again; and even on the march it forms a conspicuous feature in your baggage. A sleeping-sack, on the other hand, is always ready – you have only to get into it; it serves a double purpose – a bed by night, a portmanteau by day; and it does not advertise your intention of camping out to every curious passer-by. This is a huge point. If a camp is not secret, it is but a troubled resting-place; you become a public character; the convivial rustic visits your bedside after an early supper; and you must sleep with one eye open, and be up before the day. I decided on a sleeping-sack; and after repeated visits to Le Puy, and a deal of high living for myself and my advisers, a sleeping-sack was designed, constructed, and triumphantly brought home.

This child of my invention was nearly six feet square, exclusive of two triangular flaps to serve as a pillow by night and as the top and bottom of the sack by day. I call it 'the sack,' but it was never a sack by more than courtesy: only a sort of long roll or sausage, green waterproof cart-cloth without and blue sheep's fur within. It was commodious as a valise, warm and dry for a bed. There was luxurious turning room for one; and at a pinch the thing might serve for two.

I could bury myself in it up to the neck; for my head I trusted to a fur cap, with a hood to fold down over my ears and a band to pass under my nose like a respirator; and in case of heavy rain I proposed to make myself a little tent, or tentlet, with my waterproof coat, three stones, and a bent branch.

It will readily be conceived that I could not carry this huge package on my own, merely human, shoulders. It remained to choose a beast of burden. Now, a horse is a fine lady among animals, flighty, timid, delicate in eating, of tender health; he is too valuable and too restive to be left alone, so that you are chained to your brute as to a fellow galley-slave; a dangerous road puts him out of his wits; in short, he's an uncertain and exacting ally, and adds thirty-fold to the troubles of the voyager. What I required was something cheap and small and hardy, and of a stolid and peaceful temper; and all these requisites pointed to a donkey.

There dwelt an old man in Monastier, of rather unsound intellect according to some, much followed by street-boys, and known to fame as Father Adam. Father Adam had a cart, and to draw the cart a diminutive she-ass, not much bigger than a dog, the colour of a mouse, with a kindly eye and a determined under-jaw. There was something neat and high-bred, a quakerish elegance, about the rogue that hit my fancy on the spot. Our first interview was in Monastier market-place. To prove her good temper, one child after another was set upon her back to ride, and one after another went head over heels into the air; until a want of confidence began to reign in youthful bosoms, and the experiment was discontinued from a dearth of sub-

Le Monastier; Grand Suc de Breysse – Petit Suc de Breysse by Robert Louis Stevenson.

jects. I was already backed by a deputation of my friends; but as if this were not enough, all the buyers and sellers came round and helped me in the bargain; and the ass and I and Father Adam were the centre of a hubbub for near half an hour. At length she passed into my service for the consideration of sixty-five francs and a glass of brandy. The sack had already cost eighty francs and two glasses of beer; so that Modestine, as I instantly baptized her, was upon all accounts the cheaper article. Indeed, that was as it should be; for she was only an appurtenance of my mattress, or self-acting bedstead on four castors.

I had a last interview with Father Adam in a billiard-room at the witching hour of dawn, when I administered the brandy. He professed himself greatly touched by the separation, and declared he had often bought white bread for the donkey when he had been content with black bread for himself; but this, according to the best authorities, must have been a flight of fancy. He had a name in the village for brutally misusing the ass; yet it is certain that he shed a tear, and the tear made a clean mark down one cheek.

By the advice of a fallacious local saddler, a leather pad was made for me with rings to fasten on my bundle; and I thoughtfully completed my kit and arranged my toilette. By way of armoury and utensils, I took a revolver, a little spirit-lamp and pan, a lantern and some halfpenny candles, a jack-knife and a large leather flask. The main cargo consisted of two entire changes of warm clothing – besides my travelling wear of country velveteen, pilot-coat, and knitted spencer – some books, and my railway-rug, which, being also in the form of a bag, made me a double castle for cold nights. The permanent larder was represented by cakes of chocolate and tins of Bologna sausage. All this, except what I carried about my person, was easily stowed into the sheepskin bag; and by good fortune I threw in my empty knapsack, rather for convenience of carriage than from any thought that I should want it on my journey. For more immediate needs I took a leg of cold mutton, a bottle of Beaujolais, an empty bottle to carry milk, an egg-beater, and a considerable quantity of black bread and white, like Father Adam, for myself and donkey, only in my scheme of things the destinations were reversed.

Monastrians, of all shades of thought in politics, had agreed in threatening me with many ludicrous misadventures, and with sudden death in many surprising forms. Cold, wolves, robbers, above all the nocturnal practical joker, were daily and eloquently forced on my attention. Yet in these vaticinations, the true, patent danger was left out. Like Christian, it was from my pack I suffered by the way. Before telling my own mishaps, let me in two words relate the lesson of my experience. If the pack is well strapped at the ends, and hung at full length – not doubled, for your life – across the pack-saddle, the traveller is safe. The saddle will certainly not fit, such is the imperfection of our transitory life; it will assuredly topple and tend to overset; but there are stones on every roadside, and a man soon learns the art of correcting any tendency to overbalance with a well-adjusted stone.

A saddler sitting outside his workshop surrounded by fishing nets, horse-collars and harnesses.

On the day of my departure I was up a little after five; by six, we began to load the donkey; and ten minutes after, my hopes were in the dust. The pad would not stay on Modestine's back for half a moment. I returned it to its maker, with whom I had so contumelious a passage that the street outside was crowded from wall to wall with gossips looking on and listening. The pad changed hands with much vivacity; perhaps it would be more descriptive to say that we threw it at each other's heads; and, at any rate, we were very warm and unfriendly, and spoke with a deal of freedom.

I had a common donkey pack-saddle – a *barde,* as they call it – fitted upon Modestine; and once more loaded her with my effects. The doubled sack, my pilot-coat (for it was warm, and I was to walk in my waistcoat), a great bar of black bread, and an open basket containing the white bread, the mutton, and the bottles, were all corded together in a very elaborate system of knots, and I looked on the result with fatuous content. In such a monstrous deck-cargo, all poised above the donkey's shoulders, with nothing below to balance, on a brand-new pack-saddle that had not yet been worn to fit the animal, and fastened with brand-new girths that might be expected to stretch and slacken by the way, even a very careless traveller should have seen disaster brewing. That elaborate system of knots, again, was the work of too many sympathizers to be very artfully designed. It is true they tightened the cords with a will; as many as three at a time would have a foot against Modestine's quarters, and be hauling with clenched teeth; but I learned afterwards that one thoughtful person, without any exercise of force, can make a more solid job than half-a-dozen heated and enthusiastic grooms. I was then but a novice; even after the misadventure of the pad nothing could disturb my security, and I went forth from the stable-door as an ox goeth to the slaughter.

The Green Donkey-driver

THE bell of Monastier was just striking nine as I got quit of these preliminary troubles and descended the hill through the common. As long as I was within sight of the windows, a secret shame and the fear of some laughable defeat withheld me from tampering with Modestine. She tripped along upon her four small hoofs with a sober daintiness of gait; from time to time she shook her ears or her tail; and she looked so small under the bundle that my mind misgave me. We got across the ford without difficulty – there was no doubt about the matter, she was docility itself – and once on the other bank, where the road begins to mount through pine-woods, I took in my right hand the unhallowed staff, and with a quaking spirit applied it to the donkey. Modestine brisked up her pace for perhaps three steps, and then relapsed into her former minuet. Another application had the same effect, and so with the third. I am worthy the name of an Englishman, and it goes against my conscience to lay my hand rudely on a female. I desisted, and looked her all over from head to foot; the poor brute's knees were trembling and her breathing was distressed; it was plain that she could go no faster on a hill. God forbid, thought I, that

A typical Auvergne village painted by René Vallette. He specialised in painting scenes of various regions.

I should brutalize this innocent creature; let her go at her own pace, and let me patiently follow.

What that pace was, there is no word mean enough to describe; it was something as much slower than a walk as a walk is slower than a run; it kept me hanging on each foot for an incredible length of time; in five minutes it exhausted the spirit and set up a fever in all the muscles of the leg. And yet I had to keep close at hand and measure my advance exactly upon hers; for if I dropped a few yards into the rear, or went on a few yards ahead, Modestine came instantly to a halt and began to browse. The thought that this was to last from here to Alais nearly broke my heart. Of all conceivable journeys, this promised to be the most tedious. I tried to tell myself it was a lovely day; I tried to charm my foreboding spirit with tobacco; but I had a vision ever present to me of the long, long roads, up hill and down dale, and a pair of figures ever infinitesimally moving, foot by foot, a yard to the minute, and, like things enchanted in a nightmare, approaching no nearer to the goal.

In the meantime there came up behind us a tall peasant, perhaps forty years of age, of an ironical snuffy countenance, and arrayed in the green tail-coat of the country. He overtook us hand over hand, and stopped to consider our pitiful advance.

'Your donkey,' says he, 'is very old?'

I told him, I believed not.

Then, he supposed, we had come far.

I told him, we had but newly left Monastier.

'*Et vous marchez comme ça!*' cried he; and, throwing back his head, he laughed long and heartily. I watched him, half prepared to feel

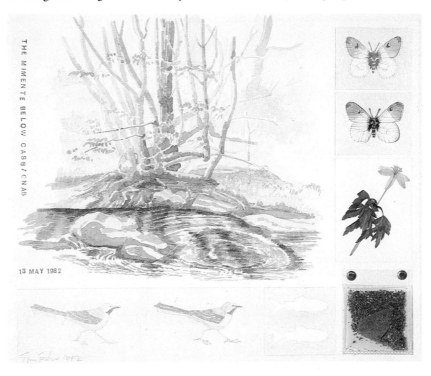

THE MIMENTE BELOW CASSICNAS

13 MAY 1982

Tony Foster is a landscape painter who creates assemblages using real objects such as flowers and stones combining them with watercolours of the scenery and wildlife. He followed Stevenson's walk in the Cévennes. This assemblage shows the Mimente below Cassagnes.

45

offended, until he had satisfied his mirth; and then, 'You must have no pity on these animals,' said he; and, plucking a switch out of a thicket, he began to lace Modestine about the sternworks, uttering a cry. The rogue pricked up her ears and broke into a good round pace, which she kept up without flagging, and without exhibiting the least symptom of distress, as long as the peasant kept beside us. Her former panting and shaking had been, I regret to say, a piece of comedy.

My *deus ex machina,* before he left me, supplied some excellent, if inhumane, advice; presented me with the switch, which he declared she would feel more tenderly than my cane; and finally taught me the true cry or masonic word of donkey-drivers, 'Proot!' All the time, he regarded me with a comical, incredulous air, which was embarrassing to confront; and smiled over my donkey-driving, as I might have smiled over his orthography, or his green tail-coat. But it was not my turn for the moment.

I was proud of my new lore, and thought I had learned the art to perfection. And certainly Modestine did wonders for the rest of the forenoon, and I had a breathing space to look about me. It was Sabbath; the mountain-fields were all vacant in the sunshine; and as we came down through St. Martin de Frugères, the church was crowded to the door, there were people kneeling without upon the steps, and the sound of the priest's chanting came forth out of the dim interior. It gave me a home feeling on the spot; for I am a country-man of the Sabbath, so to speak, and all Sabbath observances, like a Scottish accent, strike in me mixed feelings, grateful and the reverse. It is only a traveller, hurrying by like a person from another planet, who can rightly enjoy the peace and beauty of the great ascetic feast. The sight of the resting country does his spirit good. There is something better than music in the wide unusual silence; and it disposes him to amiable thoughts, like the sound of a little river or the warmth of sunlight.

In this pleasant humour I came down the hill to where Goudet stands in a green end of a valley, with Château Beaufort opposite upon a rocky steep, and the stream, as clear as crystal, lying in a deep pool between them. Above and below, you may hear it wimpling over the stones, an amiable stripling of a river, which it seems absurd to call the Loire. On all sides, Goudet is shut in by mountains; rocky foot-paths, practicable at best for donkeys, join it to the outer world of France; and the men and women drink and swear, in their green corner, or look up at the snow-clad peaks in winter from the threshold of their homes, in an isolation, you would think, like that of Homer's Cyclops. But it is not so; the postman reaches Goudet with the letter-bag; the aspiring youth of Goudet are within a day's walk of the railway at Le Puy; and here in the inn you may find an engraved portrait of the host's nephew, Régis Senac, 'Professor of Fencing and Champion of the two Americas,' a distinction gained by him, along with the sum of five hundred dollars, at Tammany Hall, New York, on the 10th April, 1876.

A sketch by Robert Louis Stevenson showing Château Beaufort from Goudet-sur-Loire.

Chateau Beaufort from Goudet sur Loire.

I hurried over my mid-day meal, and was early forth again. But, alas, as we climbed the interminable hill upon the other side, 'Proot!' seemed to have lost its virtue. I prooted like a lion, I prooted mellifluously like a sucking-dove; but Modestine would be neither softened nor intimidated. She held doggedly to her pace; nothing but a blow would move her, and that only for a second. I must follow at her heels, incessantly belabouring. A moment's pause in this ignoble toil, and she relapsed into her own private gait. I think I never heard of anyone in as mean a situation. I must reach the lake of Bouchet, where I meant to camp, before sundown, and, to have even a hope of this, I must instantly maltreat this uncomplaining animal. The sound of

Old houses of the Auvergne by René Vallette.

my own blows sickened me. Once, when I looked at her, she had a faint resemblance to a lady of my acquaintance who formerly loaded me with kindness; and this increased my horror of my cruelty.

To make matters worse, we encountered another donkey, ranging at will upon the roadside; and this other donkey chanced to be a gentleman. He and Modestine met nickering for joy, and I had to separate the pair and beat down their young romance with a renewed and feverish bastinado. If the other donkey had had the heart of a male under his hide, he would have fallen upon me tooth and hoof; and this was a kind of consolation – he was plainly unworthy of Modestine's affection. But the incident saddened me, as did everything that spoke of my donkey's sex.

It was blazing hot up the valley, windless, with vehement sun upon my shoulders; and I had to labour so consistently with my stick that the sweat ran into my eyes. Every five minutes, too, the pack, the basket, and the pilot-coat would take an ugly slew to one side or the other; and I had to stop Modestine, just when I had got her to a tolerable pace of about two miles an hour, to tug, push, shoulder, and readjust the load. And at last, in the village of Ussel, saddle and all, the whole hypothec turned round and grovelled in the dust below the donkey's belly. She, none better pleased, incontinently drew up and seemed to smile; and a party of one man, two women, and two children came up, and, standing round me in a half-circle, encouraged her by their example.

I had the devil's own trouble to get the thing righted; and the instant I had done so, without hesitation, it toppled and fell down upon the other side. Judge if I was hot! And yet not a hand was offered to assist me. The man, indeed, told me I ought to have a package of a different shape. I suggested, if he knew nothing better to the point in my predicament, he might hold his tongue. And the good-natured dog agreed with me smilingly. It was the most despicable fix. I must plainly content myself with the pack for Modestine, and take the following items for my own share of the portage: a cane, a quart flask, a pilot-jacket heavily weighted in the pockets, two pounds of black bread, and an open basket full of meats and bottles. I believe I may say I am not devoid of greatness of soul; for I did not recoil from this infamous burden. I disposed it, Heaven knows how, so as to be mildly portable, and then proceeded to steer Modestine through the village. She tried, as was indeed her invariable habit, to enter every house and every courtyard in the whole length; and, encumbered as I was, without a hand to help myself, no words can render an idea of my difficulties. A priest, with six or seven others, was examining a church in process of repair, and he and his acolytes laughed loudly as they saw my plight. I remembered having laughed myself when I had seen good men struggling with adversity in the person of a jackass, and the recollection filled me with penitence. That was in my old light days, before this trouble came upon me. God knows at least that I shall never laugh again, thought I. But oh, what a cruel thing is a farce to those engaged in it!

A little out of the village, Modestine, filled with the demon, set her heart upon a by-road, and positively refused to leave it. I dropped all my bundles, and, I am ashamed to say, struck the poor sinner twice across the face. It was pitiful to see her lift her head with shut eyes, as if waiting for another blow. I came very near crying; but I did a wiser thing than that, and sat squarely down by the roadside to consider my situation under the cheerful influence of tobacco and a nip of brandy. Modestine, in the meanwhile, munched some black bread with a contrite hypocritical air. It was plain that I must make a sacrifice to the gods of shipwreck. I threw away the empty bottle destined to carry milk; I threw away my own white bread, and, disdaining to act by general average, kept the black bread for Modestine; lastly, I threw away the cold leg of mutton and the egg-whisk, although this last was dear to my heart. Thus I found room for everything in the basket, and even stowed the boating-coat on the top. By means of an end of cord I slung it under one arm; and although the cord cut my shoulder, and the jacket hung almost to the ground, it was with a heart greatly lightened that I set forth again.

I had now an arm free to thrash Modestine, and cruelly I chastised her. If I were to reach the lakeside before dark, she must bestir her little shanks to some tune. Already the sun had gone down into a windy-looking mist; and although there were still a few streaks of gold far off to the east on the hills and the black fir-woods, all was cold and grey about our onward path. An infinity of little country by-roads led hither and thither among the fields. It was the most pointless labyrinth. I could see my destination overhead, or rather the peak that dominates it; but choose as I pleased, the roads always ended by turning away from it, and sneaking back towards the valley, or northward along the margin of the hills. The failing light, the waning colour, the naked, unhomely, stony country through which I was travelling, threw me into some despondency. I promise you, the stick was not idle; I think every decent step that Modestine took must have cost me at least two emphatic blows. There was not another sound in the neighbourhood but that of my unwearying bastinado.

Suddenly, in the midst of my toils, the load once more bit the dust, and, as by enchantment, all the cords were simultaneously loosened, and the road scattered with my dear possessions. The packing was to begin again from the beginning; and as I had to invent a new and better system, I do not doubt but I lost half an hour. It began to be dusk in earnest as I reached a wilderness of turf and stones. It had the air of being a road which should lead everywhere at the same time; and I was falling into something not unlike despair when I saw two figures stalking towards me over the stones. They walked one behind the other like tramps, but their pace was remarkable. The son led the way, a tall, ill-made, sombre, Scottish-looking man; the mother followed, all in her Sunday's best, with an elegantly embroidered ribbon to her cap, and a new felt hat atop, and proffering, as she strode along with kilted petticoats, a string of obscene and blasphemous oaths.

I hailed the son, and asked him my direction. He pointed loosely west and north-west, muttered an inaudible comment, and, without slackening his pace for an instant, stalked on, as he was going, right athwart my path. The mother followed without so much as raising her head. I shouted and shouted after them, but they continued to scale the hillside, and turned a deaf ear to my outcries. At last, leaving Modestine by herself, I was constrained to run after them, hailing the while. They stopped as I drew near, the mother still cursing; and I could see she was a handsome, motherly, respectable-looking woman. The son once more answered me roughly and inaudibly, and was for setting out again. But this time I simply collared the mother, who was nearest me, and, apologising for my violence, declared that I could not let them go until they had put me on my road. They were neither of them offended – rather mollified than otherwise; told me I had only to follow them; and then the mother asked me what I wanted by the lake at such an hour. I replied, in the Scottish manner, by inquiring if she had far to go herself. She told me, with another oath, that she had an hour and a half's road before her. And then, without salutation, the pair strode forward again up the hillside in the gathering dusk.

I returned for Modestine, pushed her briskly forward, and, after a

St. Julien d'Arpaon.

sharp ascent of twenty minutes, reached the edge of a plateau. The view, looking back on my day's journey, was both wild and sad. Mount Mézenc and the peaks beyond St. Julien stood out in trenchant gloom against a cold glitter in the east; and the intervening field of hills had fallen together into one broad wash of shadow, except here and there the outline of a wooded sugar-loaf in black, here and there a white irregular patch to represent a cultivated farm, and here and there a blot where the Loire, the Gazeille, or the Laussonne wandered in a gorge.

Soon we were on a high-road, and surprise seized on my mind as I beheld a village of some magnitude close at hand; for I had been told that the neighbourhood of the lake was uninhabited except by trout. The road smoked in the twilight with children driving home cattle from the fields; and a pair of mounted stride-legged women, hat and cap and all, dashed past me at a hammering trot from the canton where they had been to church and market. I asked one of the children where I was. At Bouchet St. Nicolas, he told me. Thither, about a mile south of my destination, and on the other side of a respectable summit, had these confused roads and treacherous peasantry conducted me. My shoulder was cut, so that it hurt sharply; my arm ached liked toothache from perpetual beating; I gave up the lake and my design to camp, and asked for the *auberge*.

The old quarters of an Auvergne town by René Vallette.

I Have a Goad

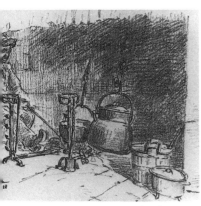

A man sitting by the fire by René Vallette.

THE *auberge* of Bouchet St. Nicolas was among the least pretentious I have ever visited; but I saw many more of the like upon my journey. Indeed, it was typical of these French highlands. Imagine a cottage of two stories, with a bench before the door; the stable and kitchen in a suite, so that Modestine and I could hear each other dining; furniture of the plainest, earthen floors, a single bedchamber for travellers, and that without any convenience but beds. In the kitchen cooking and eating go forward side by side, and the family sleep at night. Anyone who has a fancy to wash must do so in public at the common table. The food is sometimes spare; hard fish and omelette have been my portion more than once; the wine is of the smallest, the brandy abominable to man; and the visit of a fat sow, grouting under the table and rubbing against your legs, is no impossible accompaniment to dinner.

But the people of the inn, in nine cases out of ten, show themselves friendly and considerate. As soon as you cross the doors you cease to be a stranger; and although these peasantry are rude and forbidding on the highway, they show a tincture of kind breeding when you share their hearth. At Bouchet, for instance, I uncorked my bottle of Beaujolais, and asked the host to join me. He would take but little.

'I am an amateur of such wine, do you see?' he said, 'and I am capable of leaving you not enough.'

In these hedge-inns the traveller is expected to eat with his own knife; unless he ask, no other will be supplied: with a glass, a whang of bread, and an iron fork, the table is completely laid. My knife was cordially admired by the landlord of Bouchet, and the spring filled him with wonder.

'I should never have guessed that,' he said. 'I would bet,' he added, weighing it in his hand, 'that this cost you not less than five francs.'

When I told him it had cost me twenty, his jaw dropped.

He was a mild, handsome, sensible, friendly old man, astonishingly ignorant. His wife, who was not so pleasant in her manners, knew how to read, although I do not suppose she ever did so. She had a share of brains and spoke with a cutting emphasis, like one who ruled the roast.

'My man knows nothing,' she said, with an angry nod; 'he is like the beasts.'

And the old gentleman signified acquiescence with his head. There was no contempt on her part, and no shame on his; the facts were accepted loyally, and no more about the matter.

I was tightly cross-examined about my journey; and the lady understood in a moment, and sketched out what I should put into my book when I got home. 'Whether people harvest or not in such or such a place; if there were forests; studies of manners; what, for example, I and the master of the house say to you; the beauties of

A dramatic engraving showing the way through the Cévennes from Beziers to St. Pons.

Nature, and all that.' And she interrogated me with a look.

'It is just that,' said I.

'You see,' she added to her husband, 'I understood that.'

They were both much interested by the story of my misadventures.

'In the morning,' said the husband, 'I will make you something better than your cane. Such a beast as that feels nothing; it is in the proverb – *dur comme un âne*; you might beat her insensible with a cudgel, and yet you would arrive nowhere.'

Something better! I little knew what he was offering.

The sleeping-room was furnished with two beds. I had one; and I will own I was a little abashed to find a young man and his wife and child in the act of mounting into the other. This was my first experience of the sort; and if I am always to feel equally silly and extraneous, I pray God it be my last as well. I kept my eyes to myself, and know nothing of the woman except that she had beautiful arms, and seemed no whit embarrassed by my appearance. As a matter of fact, the situation was more trying to me than to the pair. A pair keep each other in countenance; it is the single gentleman who has to blush. But I could not help attributing my sentiments to the husband, and sought to conciliate his tolerance with a cup of brandy from my flask. He told me that he was a cooper of Alais travelling to St. Etienne in search of work, and that in his spare moments he followed the fatal calling of a maker of matches. Me he readily enough divined to be a brandy merchant.

I was up in the morning (Monday, September 23rd), and hastened my toilette guiltily, so as to leave a clear field for madam, the cooper's wife. I drank a bowl of milk, and set off to explore the neighbourhood of Bouchet. It was perishing cold, a grey, windy, wintry morning; misty clouds flew fast and low; the wind piped over the naked plat-form; and the only speck of colour was away behind Mount Mézenc and the eastern hills, where the sky still wore the orange of the dawn.

It was five in the morning, and four thousand feet above the sea; and I had to bury my hands in my pockets and trot. People were trooping out to the labours of the field by twos and threes, and all turned round to stare upon the stranger. I had seen them coming back last night, I saw them going afield again; and there was the life of Bouchet in a nutshell.

When I came back to the inn for a bit of breakfast, the landlady was in the kitchen combing out her daughter's hair; and I made her my compliments upon its beauty.

'Oh no,' said the mother; 'it is not so beautiful as it ought to be. Look, it is too fine.'

Thus does a wise peasantry console itself under adverse physical circumstances, and, by a startling democratic process, the defects of the majority decide the type of beauty.

'And where,' said I, 'is monsieur?'

'The master of the house is upstairs,' she answered, 'making you a goad.'

Blessed be the man who invented goads! Blessed the innkeeper of Bouchet St. Nicolas, who introduced me to their use! This plain wand, with an eighth of an inch of pin, was indeed a sceptre when he put it in my hands. Thenceforward Modestine was my slave. A prick, and she passed the most inviting stable door. A prick, and she broke forth into a gallant little trotlet that devoured the miles. It was not a remarkable speed, when all was said; and we took four hours to cover ten miles at the best of it. But what a heavenly change since yesterday! No more wielding of the ugly cudgel; no more flailing with an aching arm; no more broadsword exercise, but a discreet and gentlemanly fence. And what although now and then a drop of blood should appear on Modestine's mouse-coloured wedge-like rump? I should have preferred it otherwise, indeed; but yesterday's exploits had purged my heart of all humanity. The perverse little devil, since she would not be taken with kindness, must even go with pricking.

It was bleak and bitter cold, and, except a cavalcade of stride-legged ladies and a pair of post-runners, the road was dead solitary all the way to Pradelles. I scarce remember an incident but one. A handsome foal with a bell about his neck came charging up to us upon a stretch of common, sniffed the air martially as one about to do great deeds, and suddenly thinking otherwise in his green young heart, put about and galloped off as he had come, the bell tinkling in the wind. For a

Donkeys on the road with Stevenson and Modestine in the foreground. A drawing by Noel Rooke from an illustrated edition of 'Travels with a Donkey' published in 1912.

long while afterwards I saw his noble attitude as he drew up, and heard the note of his bell; and when I struck the high-road, the song of the telegraph-wires seemed to continue the same music.

Pradelles stands on a hillside, high above the Allier, surrounded by rich meadows. They were cutting aftermath on all sides, which gave the neighbourhood, this gusty autumn morning, an untimely smell of hay. On the opposite bank of the Allier the land kept mounting for miles to the horizon: a tanned and sallow autumn landscape, with black blots of fir-wood and white roads wandering through the hills. Over all this the clouds shed a uniform and purplish shadow, sad and somewhat menacing, exaggerating height and distance, and throwing into still higher relief the twisted ribbons of the highway. It was a cheerless prospect, but one stimulating to a traveller. For I was now

upon the limit of Velay, and all that I beheld lay in another county –
wild Gévaudan, mountainous, uncultivated, and but recently dis-
forested from terror of the wolves.

Wolves, alas, like bandits, seem to flee the traveller's advance; and
you may trudge through all our comfortable Europe, and not meet
with an adventure worth the name. But here, if anywhere, a man was
on the frontiers of hope. For this was the land of the ever-memorable
BEAST, the Napoleon Bonaparte of wolves. What a career was his!
He lived ten months at free quarters in Gévaudan and Vivarais; he
ate women and children and 'shepherdesses celebrated for their
beauty'; he pursued armed horsemen; he has been seen at broad
noonday chasing a post-chaise and outrider along the king's high-
road, and chaise and outrider fleeing before him at the gallop. He was
placarded like a political offender, and ten thousand francs were
offered for his head. And yet, when he was shot and sent to Versailles,
behold! a common wolf, and even small for that. 'Though I could
reach from pole to pole,' sang Alexander Pope; the Little Corporal
shook Europe; and if all wolves had been as this wolf, they would
have changed the history of man. M. Élie Berthet has made him the
hero of a novel, which I have read, and do not wish to read again.

Cows at Pradelles.

I hurried over my lunch, and was proof against the landlady's
desire that I should visit our Lady of Pradelles, 'who performed many
miracles, although she was of wood'; and before three-quarters of an
hour I was goading Modestine down the steep descent that leads to
Langogne on the Allier. On both sides of the road, in big dusty fields,
farmers were preparing for next spring. Every fifty yards a yoke of
great-necked stolid oxen were patiently haling at the plough. I saw
one of these mild formidable servants of the glebe, who took a sudden
interest in Modestine and me. The furrow down which he was
journeying lay at an angle to the road, and his head was solidly fixed
to the yoke like those of caryatides below a ponderous cornice; but he
screwed round his big honest eyes and followed us with a ruminating
look, until his master bade him turn the plough and proceed to
reascend the field. From all these furrowing ploughshares, from the
feet of oxen, from a labourer here and there who was breaking the dry
clods with a hoe, the wind carried away a thin dust like so much
smoke. It was a fine, busy, breathing, rustic landscape; and as I continued to descend, the highlands of Gévaudan kept mounting in front
of me against the sky.

I had crossed the Loire the day before; now I was to cross the
Allier; so near are these two confluents in their youth. Just at the
bridge of Langogne, as the long-promised rain was beginning to fall,
a lassie of some seven or eight addressed me in the sacramental
phrase, '*D'où 'st-ce-que vous venez?*' She did it with so high an air that
she set me laughing; and this cut her to the quick. She was evidently
one who reckoned on respect, and stood looking after me in silent
dudgeon, as I crossed the bridge and entered the county of Gévaudan.

Upper Gévaudan

The way also here was very wearisome through dirt and slabbiness;
nor was there on all this ground so much as one inn or victualling-
house wherein to refresh the feebler sort.
PILGRIM'S PROGRESS

──*A Camp in the Dark*──

Le Cheylard l'Évêque as seen by James Ravilious. Stevenson couldn't understand why anyone should want to visit this village.

THE next day (Tuesday, September 24th), it was two o'clock in the afternoon before I got my journal written up and my knapsack repaired, for I was determined to carry my knapsack in the future and have no more ado with baskets; and half an hour afterwards I set out for Le Cheylard l'Évêque, a place on the borders of the forest of Mercoire. A man, I was told, should walk there in an hour and a half; and I thought it scarce too ambitious to suppose that a man encumbered with a donkey might cover the same distance in four hours.

All the way up the long hill from Langogne it rained and hailed alternately; the wind kept freshening steadily, although slowly; plentiful hurrying clouds – some dragging veils of straight rain-shower, others massed and luminous as though promising snow – careered out of the north and followed me along my way. I was soon out of the cultivated basin of the Allier, and away from the ploughing oxen, and such-like sights of the country. Moor, heathery marsh, tracts of rock and pines, woods of birch all jewelled with the autumn yellow, here and there a few naked cottages and bleak fields, – these were the characters of the country. Hill and valley followed valley and hill; the little green and stony cattle-tracks wandered in and out of one another, split into three or four, died away in marshy hollows, and

began again sporadically on hillsides or at the borders of a wood.

There was no direct road to Cheylard, and it was no easy affair to make a passage in this uneven country and through this intermittent labyrinth of tracks. It must have been about four when I struck Sagnerousse, and went on my way rejoicing in a sure point of departure. Two hours afterwards, the dusk rapidly falling, in a lull of the wind, I issued from a fir-wood where I had long been wandering, and found, not the looked-for village, but another marish bottom among rough-and-tumble hills. For some time past I had heard the ringing of cattle-bells ahead; and now, as I came out of the skirts of the wood, I saw near upon a dozen cows and perhaps as many more black figures, which I conjectured to be children, although the mist had almost unrecognisably exaggerated their forms. These were all silently following each other round and round in a circle, now taking hands, now breaking up with chains and reverences. A dance of children appeals to very innocent and lively thoughts; but, at nightfall on the marshes, the thing was eerie and fantastic to behold. Even I, who am well enough read in Herbert Spencer, felt a sort of silence fall for an instant on my mind. The next I was pricking Modestine forward, and guiding her like an unruly ship through the open. In a path, she went doggedly ahead of her own accord, as before a fair wind; but once on the turf or among heather, and the brute became demented. The tendency of lost travellers to go round in a circle was developed in her to the degree of passion, and it took all the steering I had in me to keep even a decently straight course through a single field.

While I was thus desperately tacking through the bog, children and cattle began to disperse, until only a pair of girls remained behind. From these I sought direction on my path. The peasantry in general were but little disposed to counsel a wayfarer. One old devil simply retired into his house, and barricaded the door on my approach; and I might beat and shout myself hoarse, he turned a deaf ear. Another, having given me a direction which, as I found afterwards, I had misunderstood, complacently watched me going wrong without adding a sign. He did not care a stalk of parsley if I wandered all night upon the hills! As for these two girls, they were a pair of impudent sly sluts, with not a thought but mischief. One put out her tongue at me, the other bade me follow the cows, and they both giggled and jogged each other's elbows. The Beast of Gévaudan ate about a hundred children of this district; I began to think of him with sympathy.

Leaving the girls, I pushed on through the bog, and got into another wood and upon a well-marked road. It grew darker and darker. Modestine, suddenly beginning to smell mischief, bettered the pace of her own accord, and from that time forward gave me no trouble. It was the first sign of intelligence I had occasion to remark in her. At the same time, the wind freshened into half a gale, and another heavy discharge of rain came flying up out of the north. At the other side of the wood I sighted some red windows in the dusk.

An early engraving showing the wildness of the countryside.

This was the hamlet of Fouzilhic; three houses on a hillside, near a wood of birches. Here I found a delightful old man, who came a little way with me in the rain to put me safely on the road for Cheylard. He would hear of no reward, but shook his hands above his head almost as if in menace, and refused volubly and shrilly, in unmitigated *patois*.

All seemed right at last. My thoughts began to turn upon dinner and a fireside, and my heart was agreeably softened in my bosom. Alas, and I was on the brink of new and greater miseries. Suddenly, at a single swoop, the night fell. I have been abroad in many a black night, but never in a blacker. A glimmer of rocks, a glimmer of the track where it was well beaten, a certain fleecy density, or night within night, for a tree, – this was all that I could discriminate. The sky was simply darkness overhead; even the flying clouds pursued their way invisibly to human eyesight. I could not distinguish my hand at arm's-length from the track, nor my goad, at the same distance, from the meadows or the sky.

Soon the road that I was following split, after the fashion of the country, into three or four in a piece of rocky meadow. Since Modestine had shown such a fancy for beaten roads, I tried her instinct in this predicament. But the instinct of an ass is what might be expected

from the name; in half a minute she was clambering round and round among some boulders, as lost a donkey as you would wish to see. I should have camped long before had I been properly provided; but as this was to be so short a stage, I had brought no wine, no bread for myself, and little over a pound for my lady friend. Add to this, that I and Modestine were both handsomely wetted by the showers. But now, if I could have found some water, I should have camped at once in spite of all. Water, however, being entirely absent, except in the form of rain, I determined to return to Fouzilhic, and ask a guide a little farther on my way – 'a little farther lend thy guiding hand.'

The thing was easy to decide, hard to accomplish. In this sensible roaring blackness I was sure of nothing but the direction of the wind. To this I set my face. The road had disappeared, and I went across country, now in marshy opens, now baffled by walls unscalable to Modestine, until I came once more in sight of some red windows. This time they were differently disposed. It was not Fouzilhic, but Fouzilhac, a hamlet little distant from the other in space, but worlds away in the spirit of its inhabitants. I tied Modestine to a gate, and groped forward, stumbling among rocks, plunging mid-leg in bog, until I gained the entrance of the village. In the first lighted house there was a woman who would not open to me. She could do nothing, she cried to me through the door, being alone and lame; but if I would apply at the next house, there was a man who could help me if he had a mind.

They came to the next door in force, a man, two women, and a girl, and brought a pair of lanterns to examine the wayfarer. The man was not ill-looking, but had a shifty smile. He leaned against the doorpost, and heard me state my case. All I asked was a guide as far as Cheylard.

'*C'est que, voyez-vous, il fait noir,*' said he.

I told him that was just my reason for requiring help.

'I understand that,' said he, looking uncomfortable; '*mais – c'est – de la peine.*'

I was willing to pay, I said. He shook his head. I rose as high as ten francs; but he continued to shake his head.

'Name your own price, then,' said I.

'*Ce n'est pas ça,*' he said at length, and with evident difficulty; 'but I am not going to cross the door – *mais je ne sortirai pas de la porte.*'

I grew a little warm, and asked him what he proposed that I should do.

'Where are you going beyond Cheylard?' he asked by way of answer.

'That is no affair of yours,' I returned, for I was not going to indulge his bestial curiosity; 'it changes nothing in my present predicament.'

'*C'est vrai, ça,*' he acknowledged, with a laugh; '*oui, c'est vrai. Et d'où venez-vous?*'

A better man than I might have felt nettled.

'Oh,' said I, 'I am not going to answer any of your questions, so you may spare yourself the trouble of putting them. I am late enough already; I want help. If you will not guide me yourself, at least help me to find someone else who will.'

'Hold on,' he cried suddenly. 'Was it not you who passed in the meadow while it was still day?'

'Yes, yes,' said the girl, whom I had not hitherto recognised; 'it was monsieur; I told him to follow the cow.'

'As for you, mademoiselle,' said I, 'you are a *farceuse*.'

'And,' added the man, 'what the devil have you done to be still here?'

What the devil, indeed! But there I was.

'The great thing,' said I, 'is to make an end of it;' and once more proposed that he should help me to find a guide.

'*C'est que*,' he said again, '*c'est que – il fait noir*.'

'Very well,' said I; 'take one of your lanterns.'

'No,' he cried, drawing a thought backward, and again intrenching himself behind one of his former phrases; 'I will not cross the door.'

I looked at him. I saw unaffected terror struggling on his face with unaffected shame; he was smiling pitifully and wetting his lip with his tongue, like a detected schoolboy. I drew a brief picture of my state, and asked him what I was to do.

'I don't know,' he said; 'I will not cross the door.'

Here was the Beast of Gévaudan, and no mistake.

'Sir,' said I, with my most commanding manners, 'you are a coward.'

And with that I turned my back upon the family party, who hastened to retire within their fortifications; and the famous door was closed again, but not till I had overheard the sound of laughter. *Filia barbara pater barbarior.* Let me say it in the plural: the Beasts of Gévaudan.

The lanterns had somewhat dazzled me, and I ploughed distressfully among stones and rubbish-heaps. All the other houses in the village were both dark and silent; and though I knocked at here and there a door, my knocking was unanswered. It was a bad business; I gave up Fouzilhac with my curses. The rain had stopped, and the wind, which still kept rising, began to dry my coat and trousers. 'Very well,' thought I, 'water or no water, I must camp.' But the first thing was to return to Modestine. I am pretty sure I was twenty minutes groping for my lady in the dark; and if it had not been for the unkindly services of the bog, into which I once more stumbled, I might have still been groping for her at the dawn. My next business was to gain the shelter of a wood, for the wind was cold as well as boisterous. How, in this well-wooded district, I should have been so long in finding one, is another of the insoluble mysteries of this day's adventures; but I will take my oath that I put near an hour to the discovery.

At last black trees began to show upon my left, and, suddenly crossing the road, made a cave of unmitigated blackness right in front.

I call it a cave without exaggeration; to pass below that arch of leaves was like entering a dungeon. I felt about until my hand encountered a stout branch, and to this I tied Modestine, a haggard, drenched, desponding donkey. Then I lowered my pack, laid it along the wall on the margin of the road, and unbuckled the straps. I knew well enough where the lantern was; but where were the candles? I groped and groped among the tumbled articles, and, while I was thus groping, suddenly I touched the spirit-lamp. Salvation! This would serve my turn as well. The wind roared unwearyingly among the trees; I could hear the boughs tossing and the leaves churning through half a mile of forest; yet the scene of my encampment was not only as black as the pit, but admirably sheltered. At the second match the wick caught flame. The light was both livid and shifting; but it cut me off from the universe, and doubled the darkness of the surrounding night.

I tied Modestine more conveniently for herself, and broke up half the black bread for her supper, reserving the other half against the morning. Then I gathered what I should want within reach, took off my wet boots and gaiters, which I wrapped in my waterproof, arranged my knapsack for a pillow under the flap of my sleeping-bag, insulated my limbs into the interior, and buckled myself in like a *bambino*. I opened a tin of Bologna sausage and broke a cake of chocolate, and that was all I had to eat. It may sound offensive, but I ate them together, bite by bite, by way of bread and meat. All I had to wash down this revolting mixture was neat brandy: a revolting beverage in itself. But I was rare and hungry; ate well, and smoked one of the best cigarettes in my experience. Then I put a stone in my straw hat, pulled the flap of my fur cap over my neck and eyes, put my revolver ready to my hand, and snuggled well down among the sheepskins.

I questioned at first if I were sleepy, for I felt my heart beating faster than usual, as if with an agreeable excitement to which my mind remained a stranger. But as soon as my eyelids touched, that subtle glue leaped between them, and they would no more come separate. The wind among the trees was my lullaby. Sometimes it sounded for minutes together with a steady, even rush, not rising nor abating; and again it would swell and burst like a great crashing breaker, and the trees would patter me all over with big drops from the rain of the afternoon. Night after night, in my own bedroom in the country, I have given ear to this perturbing concert of the wind among the woods; but whether it was a difference in the trees, or the lie of the ground, or because I was myself outside and in the midst of it, the fact remains that the wind sang to a different tune among these woods of Gévaudan. I hearkened and hearkened: and meanwhile sleep took gradual possession of my body and subdued my thoughts and senses; but still my last waking effort was to listen and distinguish, and my last conscious state was one of wonder at the foreign clamour in my ears.

Twice in the course of the dark hours – once when a stone galled me underneath the sack, and again when the poor patient Modestine, growing angry, pawed and stamped upon the road – I was recalled for a brief while to consciousness, and saw a star or two overhead, and the lace-like edge of the foliage against the sky. When I awoke for the third time (Wednesday, September 25th), the world was flooded with a blue light, the mother of the dawn. I saw the leaves labouring in the wind and the ribbon of the road; and, on turning my head, there was Modestine tied to a beech, and standing half across the path in an attitude of inimitable patience. I closed my eyes again, and set to thinking over the experience of the night. I was surprised to find how easy and pleasant it had been, even in this tempestuous weather. The stone which annoyed me would not have been there, had I not been forced to camp blindfold in the opaque night; and I had felt no other inconvenience, except when my feet encountered the lantern or the second volume of Peyrat's *Pastors of the Desert* among the mixed contents of my sleeping-bag; nay, more, I had felt not a touch of cold, and awakened with unusually lightsome and clear sensations.

With that, I shook myself, got once more into my boots and gaiters, and, breaking up the rest of the bread for Modestine, strolled about to see in what part of the world I had awakened. Ulysses, left on

A picturesque old house with a balcony facing the sun.

Ithaca, and with a mind unsettled by the goddess, was not more pleasantly astray. I have been after an adventure all my life, a pure dispassionate adventure, such as befell early and heroic voyagers: and thus to be found by morning in a random woodside nook in Gévaudan – not knowing north from south, as strange to my surroundings as the first man upon the earth, an inland castaway – was to find a fraction of my day-dreams realised. I was on the skirts of a little wood of birch, sprinkled with a few beeches; behind, it adjoined another wood of fir; and in front, it broke up and went down in open order into a shallow and meadowy dale. All around there were bare hilltops, some near, some far away, as the perspective closed or opened, but none apparently much higher than the rest. The wind huddled the trees. The golden specks of autumn in the birches tossed shiveringly. Overhead the sky was full of strings and shreds of vapour, flying, vanishing, reappearing, and turning about an axis like tumblers, as the wind hounded them through heaven. It was wild weather and famishing cold. I ate some chocolate, swallowed a mouthful of brandy, and smoked a cigarette before the cold should have time to disable my fingers. And by the time I had got all this done, and had made my pack and bound it on the pack-saddle, the day was tiptoe on the threshold of the east. We had not gone many steps along the lane, before the sun, still invisible to me, sent a glow of gold over some cloud mountains that lay ranged along the eastern sky.

The wind had us on the stern, and hurried us bitingly forward. I buttoned myself into my coat, and walked on in a pleasant frame of mind with all men, when suddenly, at a corner, there was Fouzilhic once more in front of me. Nor only that, but there was the old gentleman who had escorted me so far the night before, running out of his house at sight of me, with hands upraised in horror.

'My poor boy!' he cried, 'what does this mean?'

I told him what had happened. He beat his old hands like clappers in a mill, to think how lightly he had let me go; but when he heard of the man of Fouzilhac, anger and depression seized upon his mind.

'This time, at least,' said he, 'there shall be no mistake.'

And he limped along, for he was very rheumatic, for about half a mile, and until I was almost within sight of Cheylard, the destination I had hunted for so long.

Cheylard and Luc

CANDIDLY, it seemed little worthy of all this searching. A few broken ends of village, with no particular street, but a succession of open places heaped with logs and faggots; a couple of tilted crosses, a shrine to Our Lady of all Graces on the summit of a little hill; and all this, upon a rattling highland river, in the corner of a naked valley. What went ye out for to see? thought I to myself. But the place had a life of its own. I found a board, commemorating the liberalities of Cheylard for the past year, hung up, like a banner, in the diminutive and tottering church. In 1877, it appeared, the inhabitants subscribed forty-eight francs ten centimes for the 'Work of the Propagation of the Faith.' Some of this, I could not help hoping, would be applied to my native land. Cheylard scrapes together halfpence for the darkened souls in Edinburgh; while Balquhidder and Dunrossness bemoan the ignorance of Rome. Thus, to the high entertainment of the angels, do we pelt each other with evangelists, like schoolboys bickering in the snow.

The inn was again singularly unpretentious. The whole furniture of a not ill-to-do family was in the kitchen: the beds, the cradle, the clothes, the plate-rack, the meal-chest, and the photograph of the

Grape-pickers at the edge of a vineyard. The man has a metal container on his back while the other containers are made of wicker. Once the grapes have been collected they are put into the wooden barrels.

parish priest. There were five children, one of whom was set to its morning prayers at the stair-foot soon after my arrival, and a sixth would ere long be forthcoming. I was kindly received by these good folk. They were much interested in my misadventure. The wood in which I had slept belonged to them; the man of Fouzilhac they thought a monster of iniquity, and counselled me warmly to summon him at law – 'because I might have died.' The good wife was horror-stricken to see me drink over a pint of uncreamed milk.

'You will do yourself an evil,' she said. 'Permit me to boil it for you.'

After I had begun the morning on this delightful liquor, she having an infinity of things to arrange, I was permitted, nay requested, to

make a bowl of chocolate for myself. My boots and gaiters were hung up to dry, and, seeing me trying to write my journal on my knee, the eldest daughter let down a hinged table in the chimney-corner for my convenience. Here I wrote, drank my chocolate, and finally ate an omelette before I left. The table was thick with dust; for, as they explained, it was not used except in winter weather. I had a clear look up the vent, through brown agglomerations of soot and blue vapour, to the sky; and whenever a handful of twigs was thrown on to the fire, my legs were scorched by the blaze.

The husband had begun life as a muleteer, and when I came to charge Modestine showed himself full of the prudence of his art. 'You will have to change this package,' said he; 'it ought to be in two parts, and then you might have double the weight.'

I explained that I wanted no more weight; and for no donkey hitherto created would I cut my sleeping-bag in two.

'It fatigues her, however,' said the innkeeper; 'it fatigues her greatly on the march. Look.'

Alas, there were her two forelegs no better than raw beef on the inside, and blood was running from under her tail. They told me when I started, and I was ready to believe it, that before a few days I should come to love Modestine like a dog. Three days had passed, we had shared some misadventures, and my heart was still as cold as a potato towards my beast of burden. She was pretty enough to look at; but then she had given proof of dead stupidity, redeemed indeed by patience, but aggravated by flashes of sorry and ill-judged light-heartedness. And I own this new discovery seemed another point against her. What the devil was the good of a she-ass if she could not carry a sleeping-bag and a few necessaries? I saw the end of the fable rapidly approaching, when I should have to carry Modestine. Æsop was the man to know the world! I assure you I set out with heavy thoughts upon my short day's march.

It was not only heavy thoughts about Modestine that weighted me upon the way; it was a leaden business altogether. For first, the wind blew so rudely that I had to hold on the pack with one hand from Cheylard to Luc; and second, my road lay through one of the most beggarly countries in the world. It was like the worst of the Scottish Highlands, only worse; cold, naked, and ignoble, scant of wood, scant of heather, scant of life. A road and some fences broke the unvarying waste, and the line of the road was marked by upright pillars, to serve in time of snow.

Why any one should desire to visit either Luc or Cheylard is more than my much-inventing spirit can suppose. For my part, I travel not to go anywhere, but to go. I travel for travel's sake. The great affair is to move; to feel the needs and hitches of our life more nearly; to come down off this feather-bed of civilisation, and find the globe granite underfoot and strewn with cutting flints. Alas, as we get up in life, and are more preoccupied with our affairs, even a holiday is a thing that must be worked for. To hold a pack upon a pack-saddle against a gale out of the freezing north is no high industry, but it is one that serves to occupy and compose the mind. And when the present is so exacting, who can annoy himself about the future?

I came out at length above the Allier. A more unsightly prospect at this season of the year it would be hard to fancy. Shelving hills rose round it on all sides, here dabbled with wood and fields, there rising to peaks alternately naked and hairy with pines. The colour throughout was black or ashen, and came to a point in the ruins of the castle of Luc, which pricked up impudently from below my feet, carrying on a pinnacle a tall white statue of Our Lady, which, I heard with interest, weighed fifty quintals, and was to be dedicated on the 6th of October. Through this sorry landscape trickled the Allier and a tributary of nearly equal size, which came down to join it through a broad nude valley in Vivarais. The weather had somewhat lightened, and the clouds massed in squadron; but the fierce wind still hunted them through heaven, and cast great ungainly splashes of shadow and sunlight over the scene.

Luc itself was a straggling double file of houses wedged between hill and river. It had no beauty, nor was there any notable feature, save the old castle overhead with its fifty quintals of brand-new Madonna. But the inn was clean and large. The kitchen, with its two box-beds hung with clean check curtains, with its wide stone chimney, its chimney-shelf four yards long and garnished with lanterns and religious statuettes, its array of chests and pair of ticking clocks, was the very model of what a kitchen ought to be – a melodrama kitchen, suitable for bandits or noblemen in disguise. Nor was the scene disgraced by the landlady, a handsome, silent, dark old woman, clothed and hooded in black like a nun. Even the public bedroom had a character of its own, with the long deal tables and benches, where fifty might have dined, set out as for a harvest-home, and the three box-beds along the wall. In one of these, lying on straw and covered with a pair of table-napkins, did I do penance all night long in gooseflesh and chattering teeth, and sigh, from time to time as I awakened, for my sheepskin sack and the lee of some great wood.

An old photograph of Luc. The path on the hill to the right of the château ends up in the main street of Luc. This would have been Stevenson's approach to the village.

Our Lady of the Snows

'I behold
The House, the Brotherhood austere –
And what am I, that I am here?'
MATTHEW ARNOLD

——Father Apollinaris——

NEXT morning (Thursday, 26th September) I took the road in a new order. The sack was no longer doubled, but hung at full length across the saddle, a green sausage six feet long with a tuft of blue wool hanging out of either end. It was more picturesque, it spared the donkey, and, as I began to see, it would insure stability, blow high, blow low. But it was not without a pang that I had so decided. For although I had purchased a new cord, and made all as fast as I was able, I was yet jealously uneasy lest the flaps should tumble out and scatter my effects along the line of march.

My way lay up the bald valley of the river, along the march of Vivarais and Gévaudan. The hills of Gévaudan on the right were a little more naked, if anything, than those of Vivarais upon the left, and the former had a monopoly of a low dotty underwood that grew thickly in the gorges and died out in solitary burrs upon the shoulders and the summits. Black bricks of fir-wood were plastered here and there upon both sides, and here and there were cultivated fields. A railway ran beside the river; the only bit of railway in Gévaudan, although there are many proposals afoot and surveys being made, and even, as they tell me, a station standing ready built in Mende. A year or two hence and this may be another world. The desert is beleaguered. Now may some Languedocian Wordsworth turn the sonnet into *patois*: 'Mountains and vales and floods, heard YE that whistle?'

At a place called La Bastide I was directed to leave the river, and follow a road that mounted on the left among the hills of Vivarais, the modern Ardèche; for I was now come within a little way of my strange destination, the Trappist monastery of Our Lady of the Snows. The sun came out as I left the shelter of a pine-wood, and I beheld suddenly a fine wild landscape to the south. High rocky hills, as blue as sapphire, closed the view, and between these lay ridge upon ridge, heathery, craggy, the sun glittering on veins of rock, the underwood clambering in the hollows, as rude as God made them at the first. There was not a sign of man's hand in all the prospect; and, indeed, not a trace of his passage, save where generation after generation had walked in twisted footpaths, in and out among the beeches, and up and down upon the channelled slopes. The mists, which had hitherto beset me, were now broken into clouds, and fled swiftly and shone brightly in the sun. I drew a long breath. It was grateful to come, after so long, upon a scene of some attraction for the human heart. I own I like definite form in what my eyes are to rest upon; and if landscapes were sold, like the sheets of characters of my boyhood, one penny plain and twopence coloured, I should go the length of twopence every day of my life.

But if things had grown better to the south, it was still desolate and inclement near at hand. A spidery cross on every hilltop marked the

neighbourhood of a religious house; and a quarter of a mile beyond, the outlook southward opening out and growing bolder with every step, a white statue of the Virgin at the corner of a young plantation directed the traveller to Our Lady of the Snows. Here, then, I struck leftward, and pursued my way, driving my secular donkey before me, and creaking in my secular boots and gaiters, towards the asylum of silence.

I had not gone very far ere the wind brought to me the clanging of a bell, and somehow, I can scarce tell why, my heart sank within me at the sound. I have rarely approached anything with more unaffected terror than the monastery of Our Lady of the Snows. This it

These peasants have brought their sheep to market to be sold. The man on the left is a shepherd and wears a smock and clogs. Next to him is a horse-dealer and three women wearing traditional round hats.

is to have had a Protestant education. And suddenly, on turning a corner, fear took hold on me from head to foot – slavish, superstitious fear; and though I did not stop in my advance, yet I went on slowly, like a man who should have passed a bourne unnoticed, and strayed into the country of the dead. For there, upon the narrow new-made road, between the stripling pines, was a mediaeval friar, fighting with a barrowful of turfs. Every Sunday of my childhood I used to study the Hermits of Marco Sadeler – enchanting prints, full of wood and field and mediaeval landscapes, as large as a county, for the imagination to go a-travelling in; and here, sure enough, was one of Marco Sadeler's heroes. He was robed in white like any spectre, and the hood falling back, in the instancy of his contention with the barrow, disclosed a pate as bald and yellow as a skull. He might have been buried any time these thousand years, and all the lively parts of him resolved into earth and broken up with the farmer's harrow.

I was troubled besides in my mind as to etiquette. Durst I address a person who was under a vow of silence? Clearly not. But drawing near, I doffed my cap to him with a far-away superstitious reverence. He nodded back, and cheerfully addressed me. Was I going to the monastery? Who was I? An Englishman? Ah, an Irishman, then?

'No,' I said, 'a Scotsman.'

A Scotsman? Ah, he had never seen a Scotsman before. And he looked me all over, his good, honest, brawny countenance shining with interest, as a boy might look upon a lion or an alligator. From him I learned with disgust that I could not be received at Our Lady of the Snows; I might get a meal, perhaps, but that was all. And then, as our talk ran on, and it turned out that I was not a pedlar, but a literary man, who drew landscapes and was going to write a book, he changed his manner of thinking as to my reception (for I fear they respect persons even in a Trappist monastery), and told me I must be sure to ask for the Father Prior, and state my case to him in full.

The monastery of Our Lady of the Snows as Stevenson would have seen it at the end of the last century. It was subsequently burnt down and later rebuilt.

Father Apollinaris, 1829–1900. Stevenson met him and thought he was 'good and simple'.

On second thoughts he determined to go down with me himself; he thought he could manage for me better. Might he say that I was a geographer?

No; I thought, in the interests of truth, he positively might not.

'Very well, then' (with disappointment), 'an author.'

It appeared he had been in a seminary with six young Irishmen, all priests long since, who had received newspapers and kept him informed of the state of ecclesiastical affairs in England. And he asked me eagerly after Dr. Pusey, for whose conversion the good man had continued ever since to pray night and morning.

'I thought he was very near the truth,' he said; 'and he will reach it yet; there is so much virtue in prayer.'

He must be a stiff, ungodly Protestant who can take anything but pleasure in this kind and hopeful story. While he was thus near the subject, the good father asked me if I were a Christian; and when he found I was not, or not after his way, he glossed it over with great goodwill.

The road which we were following, and which this stalwart father had made with his own two hands within the space of a year, came to a corner, and showed us some white buildings a little farther on beyond the wood. At the same time, the bell once more sounded abroad. We were hard upon the monastery. Father Apollinaris (for that was my companion's name) stopped me.

'I must not speak to you down there,' he said. 'Ask for the Brother Porter, and all will be well. But try to see me as you go out again through the wood, where I may speak to you. I am charmed to have made your acquaintance.'

And then suddenly raising his arms, flapping his fingers, and crying out twice, 'I must not speak, I must not speak!' he ran away in front of me, and disappeared into the monastery door.

I own this somewhat ghastly eccentricity went a good way to revive my terrors. But where one was so good and simple, why should not all be alike? I took heart of grace, and went forward to the gate as fast as Modestine, who seemed to have a disaffection for monasteries, would permit. It was the first door, in my acquaintance of her, which she had not shown an indecent haste to enter. I summoned the place in form, though with a quaking heart. Father Michael, the Father Hospitaller, and a pair of brown-robed brothers came to the gate and spoke with me a while. I think my sack was the great attraction; it had already beguiled the heart of poor Apollinaris, who had charged me on my life to show it to the Father Prior. But whether it was my address, or the sack, or the idea speedily published among that part of the brotherhood who attend on strangers that I was not a pedlar after all, I found no difficulty as to my reception. Modestine was led away by a layman to the stables, and I and my pack were received into Our Lady of the Snows.

The Monks

FATHER MICHAEL, a pleasant, fresh-faced, smiling man, perhaps of thirty-five, took me to the pantry, and gave me a glass of liqueur to stay me until dinner. We had some talk, or rather I should say he listened to my prattle indulgently enough, but with an abstracted air, like a spirit with a thing of clay. And truly, when I remember that I descanted principally on my appetite, and that it must have been by that time more than eighteen hours since Father Michael had so much as broken bread, I can well understand that he would find an earthly savour in my conversation. But his manner, though superior, was exquisitely gracious; and I find I have a lurking curiosity as to Father Michael's past.

The whet administered, I was left alone for a little in the monastery garden. This is no more than the main court, laid out in sandy paths and beds of parti-coloured dahlias, and with a fountain and a black statue of the Virgin in the centre. The buildings stand around it four-square, bleak, as yet unseasoned by the years and weather, and with no other features than a belfry and a pair of slated gables. Brothers in white, brothers in brown, passed silently along the sanded alleys; and when I first came out, three hooded monks were kneeling on the terrace at their prayers. A naked hill commands the monastery upon one side, and the wood commands it on the other. It lies exposed to wind; the snow falls off and on from October to May, and sometimes lies six weeks on end; but if they stood in Eden, with a climate like heaven's, the buildings themselves would offer the same wintry and cheerless aspect; and for my part, on this wild September day, before I was called to dinner, I felt chilly in and out.

When I had eaten well and heartily, Brother Ambrose, a hearty conversible Frenchman (for all those who wait on strangers have the liberty to speak), led me to a little room in that part of the building which is set apart for *MM. les retraitants.* It was clean and white-washed, and furnished with strict necessaries, a crucifix, a bust of the late Pope, the *Imitation* in French, a book of religious meditations, and the *Life of Elizabeth Seton,* evangelist, it would appear, of North

This attractive picture by René Vallette shows a priest walking along a road.

Looking after the hens.

America and of New England in particular. As far as my experience goes, there is a fair field for some more evangelisation in these quarters; but think of Cotton Mather! I should like to give him a reading of this little work in heaven, where I hope he dwells; but perhaps he knows all that already, and much more; and perhaps he and Mrs. Seton are the dearest friends, and gladly unite their voices in the everlasting psalm. Over the table, to conclude the inventory of the room, hung a set of regulations for *MM. les retraitants*: what services they should attend, when they were to tell their beads or meditate, and when they were to rise and go to rest. At the foot was a notable N.B.: '*Le temps libre est employé à l'examen de conscience, à la confession, à faire de bonnes résolutions,*' etc. To make good resolutions, indeed! You might talk as fruitfully of making the hair grow on your head.

I had scarce explored my niche when Brother Ambrose returned. An English boarder, it appeared, would like to speak with me. I professed my willingness, and the friar ushered in a fresh, young, little Irishman of fifty, a deacon of the Church, arrayed in strict canonicals, and wearing on his head what, in default of knowledge, I can only call the ecclesiastical shako. He had lived seven years in retreat at a convent of nuns in Belgium, and now five at Our Lady of the Snows; he never saw an English newspaper; he spoke French imperfectly, and had he spoken it like a native, there was not much chance of conversation where he dwelt. With this, he was a man eminently sociable, greedy of news, and simple-minded like a child. If I was pleased to have a guide about the monastery, he was no less delighted to see an English face and hear an English tongue.

He showed me his own room, where he passed his time among breviaries, Hebrew Bibles, and the Waverley Novels. Thence he led

me to the cloisters, into the chapter-house, through the vestry, where the brothers' gowns and broad straw hats were hanging up, each with his religious name upon a board – names full of legendary suavity and interest, such as Basil, Hilarion, Raphael, or Pacifique; into the library, where were all the works of Veuillot and Chateaubriand, and the *Odes et Ballades,* if you please, and even Molière, to say nothing of innumerable fathers and a great variety of local and general historians. Thence my good Irishman took me round the workshops, where brothers bake bread, and make cartwheels, and take photographs; where one superintends a collection of curiosities, and another a gallery of rabbits. For in a Trappist monastery each monk has an occupation of his own choice, apart from his religious duties and the general labours of the house. Each must sing in the choir, if he has a voice and ear, and join in the hay-making if he has a hand to stir; but in his private hours, although he must be occupied, he may be occupied on what he likes. Thus I was told that one brother was engaged with literature; while Father Apollinaris busies himself in making roads, and the Abbot employs himself in binding books. It is not so long since this Abbot was consecrated, by the way; and on that occasion, by a special grace, his mother was permitted to enter the chapel and witness the ceremony of consecration. A proud day for her to have a son a mitred abbot; it makes you glad to think they let her in.

In all these journeyings to and fro, many silent fathers and brethren fell in our way. Usually they paid no more regard to our passage than if we had been a cloud; but sometimes the good deacon had a permission to ask of them, and it was granted by a peculiar movement of the hands, almost like that of a dog's paws in swimming, or refused by the usual negative signs, and in either case with lowered eyelids and a certain air of contrition, as of a man who was steering very close to evil.

The monks, by special grace of their Abbot, were still taking two meals a day; but it was already time for their grand fast, which begins somewhere in September and lasts till Easter, and during which they eat but once in the twenty-four hours, and that at two in the afternoon, twelve hours after they have begun the toil and vigil of the day. Their meals are scanty, but even of these they eat sparingly; and though each is allowed a small carafe of wine, many refrain from this indulgence. Without doubt, the most of mankind grossly overeat themselves; our meals serve not only for support, but as a hearty and natural diversion from the labour of life. Yet, though excess may be hurtful, I should have thought this Trappist regimen defective. And I am astonished, as I look back, at the freshness of face and cheerfulness of manner of all whom I beheld. A happier nor a healthier company I should scarce suppose that I have ever seen. As a matter of fact, on this bleak upland, and with the incessant occupation of the monks, life is of an uncertain tenure, and death no infrequent visitor, at Our Lady of the Snows. This, at least, was what was told me. But

*The present-day monastery of
Our Lady of the Snows.*

NOTRE DAME DES NEIGES

if they die easily, they must live healthily in the meantime, for they seemed all firm of flesh and high in colour; and the only morbid sign that I could observe, an unusual brilliancy of eye, was one that served rather to increase the general impression of vivacity and strength.

Those with whom I spoke were singularly sweet-tempered, with what I can only call a holy cheerfulness in air and conversation. There is a note, in the direction to visitors, telling them not to be offended at the curt speech of those who wait upon them, since it is proper to monks to speak little. The note might have been spared; to a man the hospitallers were all brimming with innocent talk, and, in my experience of the monastery, it was easier to begin than to break off a conversation. With the exception of Father Michael, who was a man of the world, they showed themselves full of kind and healthy interest in all sorts of subjects – in politics, in voyages, in my sleeping-sack – and not without a certain pleasure in the sound of their own voices.

As for those who are restricted to silence, I can only wonder how they bear their solemn and cheerless isolation. And yet, apart from any view of mortification, I can see a certain policy, not only in the exclusion of women, but in this vow of silence. I have had some experience of lay phalansteries, of an artistic, not to say a bacchanalian, character; and seen more than one association easily formed and yet more easily dispersed. With a Cistercian rule, perhaps they might have lasted longer. In the neighbourhood of women it is but a touch-and-go association that can be formed among defenceless men; the stronger electricity is sure to triumph; the dreams of boyhood, the schemes of youth, are abandoned after an interview of ten minutes, and the arts and sciences, and professional male jollity, deserted at once for two sweet eyes and a caressing accent. And next after this, the tongue is the great divider.

I am almost ashamed to pursue this worldly criticism of a religious rule: but there is yet another point in which the Trappist order appeals to me as a model of wisdom. By two in the morning the clapper goes upon the bell, and so on, hour by hour, and sometimes quarter by quarter, till eight, the hour of rest; so infinitesimally is the day divided among different occupations. The man who keeps rabbits, for example, hurries from his hutches to the chapel, the chapter-room, or the refectory, all day long: every hour he has an office to sing, a duty to perform; from two, when he rises in the dark, till eight, when he returns to receive the comfortable gift of sleep, he is upon his feet and occupied with manifold and changing business. I know many persons, worth several thousands in the year, who are not so fortunate in the disposal of their lives. Into how many houses would not the note of the monastery bell, dividing the day into manageable portions, bring peace of mind and healthful activity of body! We speak of hardships, but the true hardship is to be a dull fool, and permitted to mismanage life in our own dull and foolish manner.

From this point of view, we may perhaps better understand the monk's existence. A long novitiate and every proof of constancy of mind and strength of body is required before admission to the order; but I could not find that many were discouraged. In the photographer's studio, which figures so strangely among the outbuildings, my eye was attracted by the portrait of a young fellow in the uniform of a private of foot. This was one of the novices, who came of the age for service, and marched and drilled and mounted guard for the proper time among the garrison of Algiers. Here was a man who had surely seen both sides of life before deciding; yet as soon as he was set free from service he returned to finish his novitiate.

This austere rule entitles a man to heaven as by right. When the Trappist sickens, he quits not his habit; he lies in the bed of death as he has prayed and laboured in his frugal and silent existence; and when the Liberator comes, at the very moment, even before they have carried him in his robe to lie his little last in the chapel among continual chantings, joy-bells break forth, as if for a marriage, from the slated belfry, and proclaim throughout the neighbourhood that another soul has gone to God.

At night, under the conduct of my kind Irishman, I took my place in the gallery to hear compline and *Salve Regina*, with which the Cistercians bring every day to a conclusion. There were none of those circumstances which strike the Protestant as childish or as tawdry in the public offices of Rome. A stern simplicity, heightened by the romance of the surroundings, spoke directly to the heart. I recall the whitewashed chapel, the hooded figures in the choir, the lights alternately occluded and revealed, the strong manly singing, the silence that ensued, the sight of cowled heads bowed in prayer, and then the clear trenchant beating of the bell, breaking in to show that the last office was over and the hour of sleep had come; and when I

The monks washing up.

remember, I am not surprised that I made my escape into the court with somewhat whirling fancies, and stood like a man bewildered in the windy starry night.

But I was weary; and when I had quieted my spirits with Elizabeth Seton's memoirs – a dull work – the cold and the raving of the wind among the pines (for my room was on that side of the monastery which adjoins the woods) disposed me readily to slumber. I was wakened at black midnight, as it seemed, though it was really two in the morning, by the first stroke upon the bell. All the brothers were then hurrying to the chapel; the dead in life, at this untimely hour, were already beginning the uncomforted labours of their day. The dead in life – there was a chill reflection. And the words of a French song came back into my memory, telling of the best of our mixed existence:

> 'Que t'as de belles filles,
> Giroflé!
> Girofla!
> Que t'as de belles filles,
> L'Amour les comptera!'

And I blessed God that I was free to wander, free to hope, and free to love.

———*The Boarders*———

BUT there was another side to my residence at Our Lady of the Snows. At this late season there were not many boarders; and yet I was not alone in the public part of the monastery. This itself is hard by the gate, with a small dining-room on the ground-floor and a whole corridor of cells similar to mine upstairs. I have stupidly forgotten the board for a regular *retraitant*; but it was somewhere between three and five francs a day, and I think most probably the first. Chance visitors like myself might give what they chose as a free-will offering, but nothing was demanded. I may mention that when I was going away, Father Michael refused twenty francs as excessive. I explained the reasoning which led me to offer him so much; but even then, from a curious point of honour, he would not accept it with his own hand.

'I have no right to refuse for the monastery,' he explained, 'but I should prefer if you would give it to one of the brothers.'

I had dined alone, because I arrived late; but at supper I found two other guests. One was a country parish priest, who had walked over that morning from the seat of his cure near Mende to enjoy four days of solitude and prayer. He was a grenadier in person, with the hale colour and circular wrinkles of a peasant; and as he complained much of how he had been impeded by his skirts upon the march, I have a vivid fancy portrait of him, striding along, upright, big-boned, with

On the road.

The monastery garden.

kilted cassock, through the bleak hills of Gévaudan. The other was a short, grizzling, thick-set man, from forty-five to fifty, dressed in tweed with a knitted spencer, and the red ribbon of a decoration in his button-hole. This last was a hard person to classify. He was an old soldier, who had seen service and risen to the rank of commandant; and he retained some of the brisk decisive manners of the camp. On the other hand, as soon as his resignation was accepted, he had come to Our Lady of the Snows as a boarder, and, after a brief experience of its ways, had decided to remain as a novice. Already the new life was beginning to modify his appearance; already he had acquired somewhat of the quiet and smiling air of the brethren; and he was yet neither an officer nor a Trappist, but partook of the character of each. And certainly here was a man in an interesting nick of life. Out of the noise of cannon and trumpets, he was in the act of passing into this still country bordering on the grave, where men sleep nightly in their grave-clothes, and, like phantoms, communicate by signs.

At supper we talked politics. I make it my business, when I am in France, to preach political good-will and moderation, and to dwell on the example of Poland, much as some alarmists in England dwell on the example of Carthage. The priest and the commandant assured me of their sympathy with all I said, and made a heavy sighing over the bitterness of contemporary feeling.

'Why, you cannot say anything to a man with which he does not absolutely agree,' said I, 'but he flies up at you in a temper.'

They both declared that such a state of things was antichristian.

While we were thus agreeing, what should my tongue stumble

upon but a word in praise of Gambetta's moderation. The old soldier's countenance was instantly suffused with blood; with the palms of his hands he beat the table like a naughty child.

'*Comment, monsieur?*' he shouted. '*Comment?* Gambetta moderate? Will you dare to justify these words?'

But the priest had not forgotten the tenor of our talk. And suddenly, in the height of his fury, the old soldier found a warning look directed on his face; the absurdity of his behaviour was brought to him in a flash; and the storm came to an abrupt end, without another word.

It was only in the morning, over our coffee (Friday, September 27th), that this couple found out I was a heretic. I suppose I had misled them by some admiring expressions as to the monastic life around us; and it was only by a point-blank question that the truth came out. I had been tolerantly used both by simple Father Apollinaris and astute Father Michael; and the good Irish deacon, when he heard of my religious weakness, had only patted me upon the shoulder and said, 'You must be a Catholic and come to heaven.' But I was now among a different sect of orthodox. These two men were bitter and upright and narrow, like the worst of Scotsmen, and indeed, upon my heart, I fancy they were worse. The priest snorted aloud like a battle-horse.

'*Et vous prétendez mourir dans cette espèce de croyance?*' he demanded; and there is no type used by mortal printers large enough to qualify his accent.

I humbly indicated that I had no design of changing.

But he could not away with such a monstrous attitude. 'No, no,' he cried; 'you must change. You have come here, God has led you here, and you must embrace the opportunity.'

I made a slip in policy; I appealed to the family affections, though I was speaking to a priest and a soldier, two classes of men circumstantially divorced from the kind and homely ties of life.

'Your father and mother?' cried the priest. 'Very well; you will convert them in their turn when you go home.'

I think I see my father's face! I would rather tackle the Gætulian lion in his den than embark on such an enterprise against the family theologian.

But now the hunt was up; priest and soldier were in full cry for my conversion; and the Work of the Propagation of the Faith, for which the people of Cheylard subscribed forty-eight francs ten centimes during 1877, was being gallantly pursued against myself. It was an odd but most effective proselytising. They never sought to convince me in argument, where I might have attempted some defence; but took it for granted that I was both ashamed and terrified at my position, and urged me solely on the point of time. Now, they said, when God had led me to Our Lady of the Snows, now was the appointed hour.

'Do not be withheld by false shame', observed the priest, for my encouragement.

A priest out visiting his parishioners.

For one who feels very similarly to all sects of religion, and who has never been able, even for a moment, to weigh seriously the merit of this or that creed on the eternal side of things, however much he may see to praise or blame upon the secular and temporal side, the situation thus created was both unfair and painful. I committed my second fault in tact, and tried to plead that it was all the same thing in the end, and we were all drawing near by different sides to the same kind and undiscriminating Friend and Father. That, as it seems to lay spirits, would be the only gospel worthy of the name. But different men think differently; and this revolutionary aspiration brought down the priest with all the terrors of the law. He launched into harrowing details of hell. The damned, he said – on the authority of a little book which he had read not a week before, and which, to add conviction to conviction, he had fully intended to bring along with him in his pocket – were to occupy the same attitude through all eternity in the midst of dismal tortures. And as he thus expatiated, he grew in nobility of aspect with his enthusiasm.

As a result the pair concluded that I should seek out the Prior, since the Abbot was from home, and lay my case immediately before him.

'*C'est mon conseil comme ancien militaire,*' observed the commandant; '*et celui de monsieur comme prêtre.*'

'*Oui,*' added the *curé,* sententiously nodding; '*comme ancien militaire – et comme prêtre.*'

At this moment, whilst I was somewhat embarrassed how to answer, in came one of the monks, a little brown fellow, as lively as a grig, and with an Italian accent, who threw himself at once into the contention, but in a milder and more persuasive vein, as befitted one of these pleasant brethren. Look at *him,* he said. The rule was very hard; he would have dearly liked to stay in his own country, Italy – it was well known how beautiful it was, the beautiful Italy; but then there were no Trappists in Italy; and he had a soul to save; and here he was.

I am afraid I must be at bottom, what a cheerful Indian critic has dubbed me, 'a faddling hedonist,' for this description of the brother's motives gave me somewhat of a shock. I should have preferred to think he had chosen the life for its own sake, and not for ulterior purposes; and this shows how profoundly I was out of sympathy with these good Trappists, even when I was doing my best to sympathise. But to the *curé* the argument seemed decisive.

'Hear that!' he cried. 'And I have seen a marquis here, a marquis, a marquis' – he repeated the holy word three times over – 'and other persons high in society; and generals. And here, at your side, is this gentleman, who has been so many years in armies – decorated, an old warrior. And here he is, ready to dedicate himself to God.'

I was by this time so thoroughly embarrassed that I pleaded cold feet, and made my escape from the apartment. It was a furious windy morning, with a sky much cleared, and long and potent intervals of sunshine; and I wandered until dinner in the wild country towards the east, sorely staggered and beaten upon by the gale, but rewarded with some striking views.

At dinner the Work of the Propagation of the Faith was recommenced, and on this occasion still more distastefully to me. The priest asked me many questions as to the contemptible faith of my fathers, and received my replies with a kind of ecclesiastical titter.

'Your sect,' he said once; 'for I think you will admit it would be doing it too much honour to call it a religion.'

'As you please, monsieur,' said I. '*La parole est à vous.*'

At length I grew annoyed beyond endurance; and although he was on his own ground and, what is more to the purpose, an old man, and so holding a claim upon my toleration, I could not avoid a protest against this uncivil usage. He was sadly discountenanced.

'I assure you,' he said, 'I have no inclination to laugh in my heart. I have no other feeling but interest in your soul.'

And there ended my conversion. Honest man! he was no dangerous deceiver; but a country parson, full of zeal and faith. Long may he tread Gévaudan with his kilted skirts – a man strong to walk and strong to comfort his parishioners in death! I daresay he would beat bravely through a snowstorm where his duty called him; and it is not always the most faithful believer who makes the cunningest apostle.

Upper Gévaudan

(continued)

The bed was made, the room was fit,
By punctual eve the stars were lit;
The air was still, the water ran;
No need there was for maid or man,
When we put up, my ass and I,
At God's green caravanserai.
OLD PLAY

Across the Goulet

A photo of La Bastide taken in 1880.

THE wind fell during dinner, and the sky remained clear; so it was under better auspices that I loaded Modestine before the monastery gate. My Irish friend accompanied me so far on the way. As we came through the wood, there was Père Apollinaris hauling his barrow; and he too quitted his labours to go with me for perhaps a hundred yards, holding my hand between both of his in front of him. I parted first from one and then from the other with unfeigned regret, but yet with the glee of the traveller who shakes off the dust of one stage before hurrying forth upon another. Then Modestine and I mounted the course of the Allier, which here led us back into Gévaudan towards its sources in the forest of Mercoire. It was but an inconsiderable burn before we left its guidance. Thence, over a hill, our way lay through a naked plateau, until we reached Chasseradès at sundown.

The company in the inn kitchen that night were all men employed in survey for one of the projected railways. They were intelligent and conversible, and we decided the future of France over hot wine, until the state of the clock frightened us to rest. There were four beds in the little upstairs room; and we slept six. But I had a bed to myself, and persuaded them to leave the window open.

'*Hé, bourgeois; il est cinq heures!*' was the cry that awakened me in the morning (Saturday, September 28th). The room was full of a transparent darkness, which dimly showed me the other three beds

and the five different nightcaps on the pillows. But out of the window
the dawn was growing ruddy in a long belt over the hill-tops, and day
was about to flood the plateau. The hour was inspiriting; and there
seemed a promise of calm weather, which was perfectly fulfilled. I
was soon under way with Modestine. The road lay for a while over
the plateau, and then descended through a precipitous village into the
valley of the Chassezac. This stream ran among green meadows, well
hidden from the world by its steep banks; the broom was in flower,
and here and there was a hamlet sending up its smoke.

At last the path crossed the Chassezac upon a bridge, and, forsaking
this deep hollow, set itself to cross the mountain of La Goulet. It
wound up through Lestampes by upland fields and woods of beech
and birch, and with every corner brought me into an acquaintance
with some new interest. Even in the gully of the Chassezac my ear
had been struck by a noise like that of a great bass bell ringing at the
distance of many miles; but this, as I continued to mount and draw
nearer to it, seemed to change in character, and I found at length that
it came from someone leading flocks afield to the note of a rural horn.
The narrow street of Lestampes stood full of sheep, from wall to wall
– black sheep and white, bleating with one accord like the birds in
spring, and each one accompanying himself upon the sheep-bell

*The courtyard of a house in the
Auvergne.*

round his neck. It made a pathetic concert, all in treble. A little higher, and I passed a pair of men in a tree with pruning-hooks, and one of them was singing the music of a *bourrée*. Still further, and when I was already threading the birches, the crowing of cocks came cheerfully up to my ears, and along with that the voice of a flute discoursing a deliberate and plaintive air from one of the upland villages. I pictured to myself some grizzled, apple-cheeked, country schoolmaster fluting in his bit of a garden in the clear autumn sunshine. All these beautiful and interesting sounds filled my heart with an unwonted expectation; and it appeared to me that, once past this range which I was mounting, I should descend into the garden of the world. Nor was I deceived, for I was now done with rains and winds and a bleak country. The first part of my journey ended here; and this was like an induction of sweet sounds into the other and more beautiful.

There are other degrees of *feyness*, as of punishment, besides the capital; and I was now led by my good spirits into an adventure which

I relate in the interest of future donkey-drivers. The road zigzagged so widely on the hillside, that I chose a short cut by map and compass, and struck through the dwarf woods to catch the road again upon a higher level. It was my one serious conflict with Modestine. She would none of my short cut; she turned in my face; she backed, she reared; she, whom I had hitherto imagined to be dumb, actually brayed with a loud hoarse flourish, like a cock crowing for the dawn. I plied the goad with one hand; with the other, so steep was the ascent, I had to hold on the pack-saddle. Half-a-dozen times she was nearly over backwards on the top of me; half-a-dozen times, from sheer weariness of spirit, I was nearly giving it up, and leading her down again to follow the road. But I took the thing as a wager, and fought it through. I was surprised, as I went on my way again, by what appeared to be chill rain-drops falling on my hand, and more than once looked up in wonder at the cloudless sky. But it was only sweat which came dropping from my brow.

St. Germain de Calberte.

Over the summit of the Goulet there was no marked road – only upright stones posted from space to space to guide the drovers. The turf underfoot was springy and well scented. I had no company but a lark or two, and met but one bullock-cart between Lestampes and Bleymard. In front of me I saw a shallow valley, and beyond that the range of the Lozère, sparsely wooded and well enough modelled in the flanks, but straight and dull in outline. There was scarce a sign of culture; only about Bleymard, the white high-road from Villefort to Mende traversed a range of meadows, set with spiry poplars, and sounding from side to side with the bells of flocks and herds.

—*A Night Among the Pines*—

FROM Bleymard after dinner, although it was already late, I set out to scale a portion of the Lozère. An ill-marked stony drove-road guided me forward; and I met nearly half-a-dozen bullock-carts descending from the woods, each laden with a whole pine-tree for the winter's firing. At the top of the woods, which do not climb very high upon this cold ridge, I struck leftward by a path among the pines, until I hit on a dell of green turf, where a streamlet made a little spout over some stones to serve me for a water-tap. 'In a more sacred or sequestered bower . . . nor nymph nor faunus haunted.' The trees were not old, but they grew thickly round the glade: there was no outlook, except north-eastward upon distant hill-tops, or straight upward to the sky; and the encampment felt secure and private like a room. By the time I had made my arrangements and fed Modestine, the day was already beginning to decline. I buckled myself to the knees into my sack and made a hearty meal; and as soon as the sun went down, I pulled my cap over my eyes and fell asleep.

Night is a dead monotonous period under a roof; but in the open world it passes lightly, with its stars and dews and perfumes, and the hours are marked by changes in the face of Nature. What seems a kind of temporal death to people choked between walls and curtains, is only a light and living slumber to the man who sleeps afield. All night long he can hear Nature breathing deeply and freely; even as she takes her rest, she turns and smiles; and there is one stirring hour unknown to those who dwell in houses, when a wakeful influence goes abroad over the sleeping hemisphere, and all the outdoor world are on their feet. It is then that the cock first crows, not this time to announce the dawn, but like a cheerful watchman speeding the course of night. Cattle awake on the meadows; sheep break their fast on dewy hillsides, and change to a new lair among the ferns; and house-less men, who have laid down with the fowls, open their dim eyes and behold the beauty of the night.

At what inaudible summons, at what gentle touch of Nature, are all these sleepers thus recalled in the same hour to life? Do the stars rain down an influence, or do we share some thrill of mother earth below our resting bodies? Even shepherds and old country-folk, who are the deepest read in these arcana, have not a guess as to the means or purpose of this nightly resurrection. Towards two in the morning they declare the thing takes place; and neither know nor inquire further. And at least it is a pleasant incident. We are disturbed in our slumber only, like the luxurious Montaigne, 'that we may the better and more sensibly relish it.' We have a moment to look upon the stars. And there is a special pleasure for some minds in the reflection that we share the impulse with all outdoor creatures in our neighbourhood, that we have escaped out of the Bastille of civilisation, and are become, for the time being, a mere kindly animal and a sheep of Nature's flock.

When that hour came to me among the pines, I wakened thirsty. My tin was standing by me half full of water. I emptied it at a draught; and feeling broad awake after this internal cold aspersion, sat upright to make a cigarette. The stars were clear, coloured, and jewel-like, but not frosty. A faint silvery vapour stood for the Milky Way. All around me the black fir-points stood upright and stock-still. By the whiteness of the pack-saddle, I could see Modestine walking round and round at the length of her tether; I could hear her steadily munching at the sward; but there was not another sound, save the indescribable quiet talk of the runnel over the stones. I lay lazily smoking and studying the colour of the sky, as we call the void of space, from where it showed a reddish grey behind the pines to where it showed a glossy blue-black between the stars. As if to be more like a pedlar, I wear a silver ring. This I could see faintly shining as I raised or lowered the cigarette; and at each whiff the inside of my hand was illuminated, and became for a second the highest light in the landscape.

A faint wind, more like a moving coolness than a stream of air, passed down the glade from time to time; so that even in my great chamber the air was being renewed all night long. I thought with

horror of the inn at Chasseradès and the congregated nightcaps; with horror of the nocturnal prowesses of clerks and students, of hot theatres and pass-keys and close rooms. I have not often enjoyed a more serene possession of myself, nor felt more independent of material aids. The outer world, from which we cower into our houses, seemed after all a gentle habitable place; and night after night a man's bed, it seemed, was laid and waiting for him in the fields, where God keeps an open house. I thought I had rediscovered one of those truths which are revealed to savages and hid from political economists: at the least, I had discovered a new pleasure for myself. And yet even while I was exulting in my solitude I became aware of a strange lack. I wished a companion to lie near me in the starlight, silent and not moving, but ever within touch. For there is a fellowship more quiet even than solitude, and which, rightly understood, is solitude made perfect. And to live out of doors with the woman a man loves is of all lives the most complete and free.

As I thus lay, between content and longing, a faint noise stole towards me through the pines. I thought, at first, it was the crowing of cocks or the barking of dogs at some very distant farm; but steadily and gradually it took articulate shape in my ears, until I became aware that a passenger was going by upon the high-road in the valley, and singing loudly as he went. There was more of good-will than grace in his performance; but he trolled with ample lungs; and the sound of his voice took hold upon the hillside and set the air shaking in the leafy glens. I have heard people passing by night in sleeping cities; some of them sang; one, I remember, played loudly on the bagpipes. I have heard the rattle of a cart or carriage spring up suddenly after hours of stillness, and pass, for some minutes, within the range of my hearing as I lay abed. There is a romance about all who are abroad in the black hours, and with something of a thrill we try to guess their business. But here the romance was double: first, this glad passenger, lit internally with wine, who sent up his voice in music through the night; and then I, on the other hand, buckled into my sack, and smoking alone in the pine-woods between four and five thousand feet towards the stars.

When I awoke again (Sunday, 29th September), many of the stars had disappeared; only the stronger companions of the night still burned visibly overhead; and away towards the east I saw a faint haze of light upon the horizon, such as had been the Milky Way when I was last awake. Day was at hand. I lit my lantern, and by its glow-worm light put on my boots and gaiters; then I broke up some bread for Modestine, filled my can at the water-tap, and lit my spirit-lamp to boil myself some chocolate. The blue darkness lay long in the glade where I had so sweetly slumbered; but soon there was a broad streak of orange melting into gold along the mountain-tops of Vivarais. A solemn glee possessed my mind at this gradual and lovely coming in of day. I heard the runnel with delight; I looked round me for something beautiful and unexpected; but the still black pine-trees, the hollow glade, the munching ass, remained unchanged in figure. Nothing had altered but the light, and that, indeed, shed over all a spirit of life and of breathing peace, and moved me to a strange exhilaration.

I drank my water-chocolate, which was hot if it was not rich, and strolled here and there, and up and down about the glade. While I was thus delaying, a gush of steady wind, as long as a heavy sigh, poured direct out of the quarter of the morning. It was cold, and set me sneezing. The trees near at hand tossed their black plumes in its passage; and I could see the thin distant spires of pine along the edge of the hill rock slightly to and fro against the golden east. Ten minutes after, the sunlight spread at a gallop along the hillside, scattering shadows and sparkles, and the day had come completely.

I hastened to prepare my pack, and tackle the steep ascent that lay before me; but I had something on my mind. It was only a fancy; yet a fancy will sometimes be importunate. I had been most hospitably received and punctually served in my green caravanserai. The room was airy, the water excellent, and the dawn had called me to a moment. I say nothing of the tapestries or the inimitable ceiling, nor yet of the view which I commanded from the windows; but I felt I was in some one's debt for all this liberal entertainment. And so it pleased me, in a half-laughing way, to leave pieces of money on the turf as I went along, until I had left enough for my night's lodging. I trust they did not fall to some rich and churlish drover.

A photograph by James Ravilious of the area around Le Cheylard l'Évêque.

The Country of the Camisards

We travelled in the print of olden wars;
Yet all the land was green;
And love we found, and peace,
Where fire and war had been.
They pass and smile, the children of the sword –
No more the sword they wield;
And O, how deep the corn
Along the battlefield!

W. P. BANNATYNE

Across the Lozère

THE track that I had followed in the evening soon died out, and I continued to follow over a bald turf ascent a row of stone pillars, such as had conducted me across the Goulet. It was already warm. I tied my jacket on the pack, and walked in my knitted waistcoat. Modestine herself was in high spirits, and broke of her own accord, for the first time in my experience, into a jolting trot that set the oats swashing in the pocket of my coat. The view, back upon the northern Gévaudan, extended with every step; scarce a tree, scarce a house, appeared upon the fields of wild hill that ran north, east, and west, all blue and gold in the haze and sunlight of the morning. A multitude of little birds kept sweeping and twittering about my path; they perched on the stone pillars, they pecked and strutted on the turf, and I saw them circle in volleys in the blue air, and show, from time to time, translucent flickering wings between the sun and me.

Almost from the first moment of my march, a faint large noise, like a distant surf, had filled my ears. Sometimes I was tempted to think it the voice of a neighbouring waterfall, and sometimes a subjective result of the utter stillness of the hill. But as I continued to advance, the noise increased, and became like the hissing of an enormous tea-urn, and at the same time breaths of cool air began to reach me from the direction of the summit. At length I understood. It was blowing stiffly from the south upon the other slope of the Lozère, and every step that I took I was drawing nearer to the wind.

Although it had been long desired, it was quite unexpectedly at last that my eyes rose above the summit. A step that seemed no way more decisive than many other steps that had preceded it – and, 'like stout Cortez when, with eagle eyes, he stared on the Pacific,' I took possession, in my own name, of a new quarter of the world. For behold, instead of the gross turf rampart I had been mounting for so long, a view into the hazy air of heaven, and a land of intricate blue hills below my feet.

The Lozère lies nearly east and west, cutting Gévaudan into two unequal parts; its highest point, this Pic de Finiels, on which I was then standing, rises upwards of five thousand six hundred feet above the sea, and in clear weather commands a view over all lower Languedoc to the Mediterranean Sea. I have spoken with people who either pretended or believed that they had seen, from the Pic de Finiels, white ships sailing by Montpellier and Cette. Behind was the upland northern country through which my way had lain, peopled by a dull race, without wood, without much grandeur of hill-form, and famous in the past for little beside wolves. But in front of me, half veiled in sunny haze, lay a new Gévaudan, rich, picturesque, illustrious for stirring events. Speaking largely, I was in the Cévennes at Monastier, and during all my journey; but there is a strict and local sense in which only this confused and shaggy country at my feet has

View from Montagne du Goulet. any title to the name, and in this sense the peasantry employ the word. These are the Cévennes with an emphasis: the Cévennes of the Cévennes. In that undecipherable labyrinth of hills, a war of bandits, a war of wild beasts, raged for two years between the Grand Monarch with all his troops and marshals on the one hand, and a few thousand Protestant mountaineers upon the other. A hundred and eighty years ago, the Camisards held a station even on the Lozère, where I stood; they had an organisation, arsenals, a military and religious hierarchy; their affairs were 'the discourse of every coffee-house' in London; England sent fleets in their support; their leaders prophesied and murdered; with colours and drums, and the singing of old French psalms, their bands sometimes affronted daylight, marched before walled cities, and dispersed the generals of the king; and sometimes at night, or in masquerade, possessed themselves of strong castles, and avenged treachery upon their allies and cruelty upon their foes. There, a hundred and eighty years ago, was the chivalrous Roland, 'Count and Lord Roland, generalissimo of the Protestants in France,' grave, silent, imperious, pock-marked ex-dragoon, whom a lady followed in his wanderings out of love. There was Cavalier, a baker's apprentice with a genius for war, elected brigadier of Camisards at seventeen, to die at fifty-five the English governor of Jersey. There again was Castanet, a partisan leader in a voluminous peruke and with a taste for controversial divinity. Strange generals, who moved apart to take counsel with the God of Hosts, and fled or offered battle, set sentinels or slept in an unguarded camp, as the Spirit whispered to their hearts! And there, to follow these and other leaders, was the rank and file of prophets and disciples, bold, patient, indefatigable, hardy to run upon the mountains, cheering their rough life with psalms, eager to fight, eager to pray, listening devoutly to the oracles of brain-sick children, and mystically putting a grain of wheat among

the pewter balls with which they charged their muskets.

I had travelled hitherto through a dull district, and in the track of nothing more notable than the child-eating beast of Gévaudan, the Napoleon Bonaparte of wolves. But now I was to go down into the scene of a romantic chapter – or, better, a romantic footnote – in the history of the world. What was left of all this bygone dust and heroism? I was told that Protestantism still survived in this head seat of Protestant resistance; so much the priest himself had told me in the monastery parlour. But I had yet to learn if it were a bare survival, or a lively and generous tradition. Again, if in the northern Cévennes the people are narrow in religious judgments, and more filled with zeal than charity, what was I to look for in this land of persecution and reprisal – in a land where the tyranny of the Church produced the Camisard rebellion, and the terror of the Camisards threw the Catholic peasantry into legalised revolt upon the other side, so that Camisard and Florentin skulked for each other's lives among the mountains?

Just on the brow of the hill, where I paused to look before me, the series of stone pillars came abruptly to an end; and only a little below, a sort of track appeared and began to go down a break-neck slope, turning like a corkscrew as it went. It led into a valley between falling hills, stubbly with rocks like a reaped field of corn, and floored farther down with green meadows. I followed the track with precipitation; the steepness of the slope, the continual agile turning of the line of the descent, and the old unwearied hope of finding something new in a new country, all conspired to lend me wings. Yet a little lower and a stream began, collecting itself together out of many fountains, and soon making a glad noise among the hills. Sometimes it would cross the track in a bit of waterfall, with a pool, in which Modestine refreshed her feet.

The whole descent is like a dream to me, so rapidly was it accomplished. I had scarcely left the summit ere the valley had closed round my path, and the sun beat upon me, walking in a stagnant lowland atmosphere. The track became a road, and went up and down in easy undulations. I passed cabin after cabin, but all seemed deserted; and

An old Auvergne house drawn by René Vallette.

Des Colquierés – St. Germain de Calberte.

I saw not a human creature, nor heard any sound except that of the stream. I was, however, in a different country from the day before. The stony skeleton of the world was here vigorously displayed to sun and air. The slopes were steep and changeful. Oak-trees clung along the hills, well grown, wealthy in leaf, and touched by the autumn with strong and luminous colours. Here and there another stream would fall in from the right or the left, down a gorge of snow-white and tumultuary boulders. The river in the bottom (for it was rapidly growing a river, collecting on all hands as it trotted on its way) here foaming a while in desperate rapids, and there lay in pools of the most enchanting sea-green shot with watery browns. As far as I have gone, I have never seen a river of so changeful and delicate a hue; crystal was not more clear, the meadows were not by half so green; and at every pool I saw I felt a thrill of longing to be out of these hot, dusty, and material garments, and bathe my naked body in the mountain air and water. All the time as I went on I never forgot it was the Sabbath; the stillness was a perpetual reminder; and I heard in spirit the church-bells clamouring all over Europe, and the psalms of a thousand churches.

At length a human sound struck my ear – a cry strangely modulated between pathos and derision; and looking across the valley, I saw a little urchin sitting in a meadow, with his hands about his knees, and dwarfed to almost comical smallness by the distance. But the rogue had picked me out as I went down the road, from oak wood on to oak wood, driving Modestine; and he made me the compliments of the new country in this tremulous high-pitched salutation. And as all noises are lovely and natural at a sufficient distance, this also, coming through so much clean hill air and crossing all the green valley, sounded pleasant to my ear, and seemed a thing rustic, like the oaks or the river.

A little after, the stream that I was following fell into the Tarn at Pont de Montvert of bloody memory.

Pont de Montvert

An old woman sitting on her steps. To the left is her house and to the right a barn. Notice that the top roof is thatched and the lower one is made of rounded tiles. The building is made of stone.

ONE of the first things I encountered in Pont de Montvert was, if I remember rightly, the Protestant temple; but this was but the type of other novelties. A subtle atmosphere distinguishes a town in England from a town in France, or even in Scotland. At Carlisle you can see you are in the one country; at Dumfries, thirty miles away, you are as sure that you are in the other. I should find it difficult to tell in what particulars Pont de Montvert differed from Monastier or Langogne,

A street scene from an old engraving.

or even Bleymard; but the difference existed, and spoke eloquently to the eyes. The place, with its houses, its lanes, its glaring river-bed, wore an indescribable air of the South.

All was Sunday bustle in the streets and in the public-house, as all had been Sabbath peace among the mountains. There must have been near a score of us at dinner by eleven before noon; and after I had eaten and drunken, and sat writing up my journal, I suppose as many more came dropping in one after another, or by twos and threes. In crossing the Lozère I had not only come among new natural features, but moved into the territory of a different race. These people, as they hurriedly despatched their viands in an intricate sword-play of knives, questioned and answered me with a degree of intelligence which excelled all that I had met, except among the railway folk at Chasseradès. They had open telling faces, and were lively both in speech and manner. They not only entered thoroughly into the spirit of my little trip, but more than one declared, if he were rich enough, he would like to set forth on such another.

Even physically there was a pleasant change. I had not seen a pretty woman since I left Monastier, and there but one. Now of the three who sat down with me to dinner, one was certainly not beautiful – a poor timid thing of forty, quite troubled at this roaring *table d'hôte*, whom I squired and helped to wine, and pledged and tried generally to encourage, with quite a contrary effect; but the other two, both married, were both more handsome than the average of women. And Clarisse? What shall I say of Clarisse? She waited the table with a heavy placable nonchalance, like a performing cow; her great grey eyes were steeped in amorous languor; her features, although fleshy, were of an original and accurate design; her mouth had a curl; her nostril spoke of dainty pride; her cheek fell into strange and interesting lines. It was a face capable of strong emotion, and, with training, it offered the promise of delicate sentiment. It seemed pitiful to see so good a model left to country admirers and a country way of thought. Beauty should at least have touched society; then, in a moment, it throws off a weight that lay upon it, it becomes conscious of itself, it puts on an elegance, learns a gait and a carriage of the head, and, in a moment, *patet dea*. Before I left I assured Clarisse of my hearty admiration. She took it like milk, without embarrassment or wonder, merely looking at me steadily with her great eyes; and I own the result upon myself was some confusion. If Clarisse could read English, I should not dare to add that her figure was unworthy of her face. Hers was a case for stays; but that may perhaps grow better as she gets up in years.

Pont de Montvert, or Greenhill Bridge, as we might say at home, is a place memorable in the story of the Camisards. It was here that the war broke out; here that those southern Covenanters slew their Archbishop Sharp. The persecution on the one hand, the febrile enthusiasm on the other, are almost equally difficult to understand in these quiet modern days, and with our easy modern beliefs and disbeliefs. The Protestants were one and all beside their right minds with zeal and sorrow. They were all prophets and prophetesses. Children at the breast would exhort their parents to good works. 'A child of fifteen months at Quissac spoke from its mother's arms, agitated and sobbing, distinctly and with a loud voice.' Marshal Villars has seen a town where all the women 'seemed possessed by the devil,' and had trembling fits, and uttered prophecies publicly upon the streets. A prophetess of Vivarais was hanged at Montpellier because blood flowed from her eyes and nose, and she declared that she was weeping tears of blood for the misfortunes of the Protestants. And it was not only women and children. Stalwart dangerous fellows, used to swing the sickle or to wield the forest axe, were likewise shaken with strange paroxysms, and spoke oracles with sobs and streaming tears. A persecution unsurpassed in violence had lasted near a score of years, and this was the result upon the persecuted; hanging, burning, breaking on the wheel, had been in vain; the dragoons had left their hoof-marks over all the countryside; there were men rowing in the galleys, and women pining in the prisons of the Church; and not a thought was changed in the heart of any upright Protestant.

Now the head and forefront of the persecution – after Lamoignon de Bâvile – François de Langlade du Chayla (pronounce Chéila), Archpriest of the Cévennes and Inspector of Missions in the same country, had a house in which he sometimes dwelt in the town of Pont de Montvert. He was a conscientious person, who seems to have been intended by nature for a pirate, and now fifty-five, an age by which a man has learned all the moderation of which he is capable.

A missionary in his youth in China, he there suffered martyrdom, was left for dead, and only succoured and brought back to life by the charity of a pariah. We must suppose the pariah devoid of second-sight, and not purposely malicious in this act. Such an experience, it might be thought, would have cured a man of the desire to persecute; but the human spirit is a thing strangely put together; and, having been a Christian martyr, Du Chayla became a Christian persecutor. The Work of the Propagation of the Faith went roundly forward in his hands. His house in Pont de Montvert served him as a prison. There he closed the hands of his prisoners upon live coal, and plucked out the hairs of their beards, to convince them that they were deceived in their opinions. And yet had not he himself tried and proved the efficiency of these carnal arguments among the Buddhists in China?

Not only was life made intolerable in Languedoc, but flight was rigidly forbidden. One Massip, a muleteer, and well acquainted with the mountain-paths, had already guided several troops of fugitives in safety to Geneva; and on him, with another convoy, consisting mostly of women dressed as men, Du Chayla, in an evil hour for himself, laid his hands. The Sunday following, there was a conventicle of

Protestants in the woods of Altefage upon Mount Bougès; where there stood up one Séguier – Spirit Séguier, as his companions called him – a wool-carder, tall, black-faced, and toothless, but a man full of prophecy. He declared, in the name of God, that the time for submission had gone by, and they must betake themselves to arms for the deliverance of their brethren and the destruction of the priests.

The next night, 24th July, 1702, a sound disturbed the Inspector of Missions as he sat in his prison-house at Port de Montvert: the voices of many men upraised in psalmody drew nearer and nearer through the town. It was ten at night; he had his court about him, priests, soldiers, and servants, to the number of twelve or fifteen; and now dreading the insolence of a conventicle below his very windows, he ordered forth his soldiers to report. But the psalm-singers were already at his door, fifty strong, led by the inspired Séguier, and breathing death. To their summons, the archpriest made answer like a stout old persecutor, and bade his garrison fire upon the mob. One Camisard (for, according to some, it was in this night's work that they came by the name) fell at this discharge: his comrades burst in the door with hatchets and a beam of wood, overran the lower story of the house, set free the prisoners, and finding one of them in the *vine*, a sort of Scavenger's Daughter of the place and period, redoubled in fury against Du Chayla, and sought by repeated assaults to carry the upper floors. But he, on his side, had given absolution to his men, and they bravely held the staircase.

'Children of God,' cried the prophet, 'hold your hands. Let us burn the house, with the priest and the satellites of Baal.'

The fire caught readily. Out of an upper window Du Chayla and his men lowered themselves into the garden by means of knotted sheets; some escaped across the river under the bullets of the insurgents; but the archpriest himself fell, broke his thigh, and could only crawl into the hedge. What were his reflections as this second martyrdom drew near? A poor, brave, besotted, hateful man, who had done his duty resolutely according to his light both in the Cévennes and China. He found at least one telling word to say in his defence; for when the roof fell in and the upbursting flames discovered his retreat, and they came and dragged him to the public place of the town, raging and calling him damned – 'If I be damned,' said he, 'why should you also damn yourselves?'

Here was a good reason for the last; but in the course of his inspectorship he had given many stronger which all told in a contrary direction; and these he was now to hear. One by one, Séguier first, the Camisards drew near and stabbed him. 'This,' they said, 'is for my father broken on the wheel. This for my brother in the galleys. That for my mother or my sister imprisoned in your cursed convents.' Each gave his blow and his reason; and then all kneeled and sang psalms around the body till the dawn. With the dawn, still singing, they defiled away towards Frugères, farther up the Tarn, to pursue the work of vengeance, leaving Du Chayla's prison-house in ruins,

Saint-André-en-Morvan 1842 by Corot. Corot made several visits to the Auvergne to paint.

and his body pierced with two-and-fifty wounds upon the public place.

'Tis a wild night's work, with its accompaniment of psalms; and it seems as if a psalm must always have a sound of threatening in that town upon the Tarn. But the story does not end, even so far as concerns Pont de Montvert, with the departure of the Camisards. The career of Séguier was brief and bloody. Two more priests and a whole family at Ladevèze, from the father to the servants, fell by his hand or by his orders; and yet he was but a day or two at large, and restrained all the time by the presence of the soldiery. Taken at length by a famous soldier of fortune, Captain Poul, he appeared unmoved before his judges.

'Your name?' they asked.

'Pierre Séguier.'

'Why are you called Spirit?'

'Because the Spirit of the Lord is with me.'

'Your domicile?'

'Lately in the desert, and soon in heaven.'

'Have you no remorse for your crimes?'

'I have committed none. *My soul is like a garden full of shelter and of fountains.*'

At Pont de Montvert, on the 12th of August, he had his right hand stricken from his body, and was burned alive. And his soul was like a garden? So perhaps was the soul of Du Chayla, the Christian martyr. And perhaps if you could read in my soul, or I could read in yours, our own composure might seem little less surprising.

Du Chayla's house still stands, with a new roof, beside one of the bridges of the town; and if you are curious you may see the terrace-garden into which he dropped.

In the Valley of the Tarn

A NEW road leads from Pont de Montvert to Florac by the valley of the Tarn; a smooth sandy ledge, it runs about half-way between the summit of the cliffs and the river in the bottom of the valley; and I went in and out, as I followed it, from bays of shadow into promontories of afternoon sun. This was a pass like that of Killiecrankie; a deep turning gully in the hills, with the Tarn making a wonderful hoarse uproar far below, and craggy summits standing in the sunshine high above. A thin fringe of ash-trees ran about the hill-tops, like ivy on a ruin; but on the lower slopes, and far up every glen, the Spanish chestnut-trees stood each four-square to heaven under its tented foliage. Some were planted, each on its own terrace no larger than a bed; some, trusting in their roots, found strength to grow and prosper and be straight and large upon the rapid slopes of the valley; others, where there was a margin to the river, stood marshalled in a line and mighty like cedars of Lebanon. Yet even where they grew most thickly they were not to be thought of as a wood, but as a herd of stalwart individuals; and the dome of each tree stood forth separate and large, and as it were a little hill, from among the domes of its companions. They gave forth a faint sweet perfume which pervaded the air of the afternoon; autumn had put tints of gold and tarnish in the green; and the sun so shone through and kindled the broad foliage, that each chestnut was relieved against another, not in shadow, but in light. A humble sketcher here laid down his pencil in despair.

I wish I could convey a notion of the growth of these noble trees; of how they strike out boughs like the oak, and trail sprays of drooping foliage like the willow; of how they stand on upright fluted columns like the pillars of a church; or like the olive, from the most shattered bole can put out smooth and youthful shoots, and begin a new life upon the ruins of the old. Thus they partake of the nature of many different trees; and even their prickly top-knots, seen near at hand against the sky, have a certain palm-like air that impresses the imagination. But their individuality, although compounded of so many elements, is but the richer and the more original. And to look down upon a level filled with these knolls of foliage, or to see a clan of old unconquerable chestnuts cluster 'like herded elephants' upon the spur of a mountain, is to rise to higher thoughts of the powers that are in Nature.

Between Modestine's laggard humour and the beauty of the scene, we made little progress all that afternoon; and at last finding the sun, although still far from setting, was already beginning to desert the narrow valley of the Tarn, I began to cast about for a place to camp in. This was not easy to find; the terraces were too narrow, and the ground, where it was unterraced, was usually too steep for a man to lie upon. I should have slipped all night, and awakened towards morning with my feet or my head in the river.

After perhaps a mile, I saw, some sixty feet above the road, a little plateau large enough to hold my sack, and securely parapeted by the trunk of an aged and enormous chestnut. Thither, with infinite trouble, I goaded and kicked the reluctant Modestine, and there I hastened to unload her. There was only room for myself upon the plateau, and I had to go nearly as high again before I found so much as standing room for the ass. It was on a heap of rolling stones, on an artificial terrace, certainly not 5 feet square in all. Here I tied her to a chestnut, and having given her corn and bread and made a pile of chestnut-leaves, of which I found her greedy, I descended once more to my own encampment.

The position was unpleasantly exposed. One or two carts went by upon the road; and as long as daylight lasted I concealed myself, for all the world like a hunted Camisard, behind my fortification of vast chestnut trunk; for I was passionately afraid of discovery and the visit of jocular persons in the night. Moreover, I saw that I must be early awake; for these chestnut gardens had been the scene of

industry no further gone than on the day before. The slope was strewn with lopped branches, and here and there a great package of leaves was propped against a trunk; for even the leaves are serviceable, and the peasants use them in winter by way of fodder for their animals. I picked a meal in fear and trembling, half lying down to hide myself from the road; and I daresay I was as much concerned as if I had been a scout from Joani's band above upon the Lozère, or from Salomon's across the Tarn, in the old times of psalm-singing and blood. Or, indeed, perhaps more; for the Camisards had a remarkable confidence in God; and a tale comes back into my memory of how the Count of Gévaudan, riding with a party of dragoons and a notary at his saddle-bow to enforce the oath of fidelity in all the country hamlets, entered a valley in the woods, and found Cavalier and his men at dinner, gaily seated on the grass, and their hats crowned with box-tree garlands, while fifteen women washed their linen in the stream. Such was a field festival in 1703; at that date Antony Watteau would be painting similar subjects.

This was a very different camp from that of the night before in the cool and silent pine-woods. It was warm and even stifling in the valley. The shrill song of frogs, like the tremolo note of a whistle with a pea in it, rang up from the riverside before the sun was down. In the growing dusk, faint rustlings began to run to and fro among the fallen leaves; from time to time a faint chirping or cheeping noise would fall upon my ear; and from time to time I thought I could see the movement of something swift and indistinct between the chestnuts. A profusion of large ants swarmed upon the ground; bats whisked by, and mosquitoes droned overhead. The long boughs with their bunches of leaves hung against the sky like garlands; and those immediately above and around me had somewhat the air of a trellis which should have been wrecked and half overthrown in a gale of wind.

Sleep for a long time fled my eyelids; and just as I was beginning to feel quiet stealing over my limbs, and settling densely on my mind, a noise at my head startled me broad awake again, and, I will frankly confess, brought my heart into my mouth. It was such a noise as a person would make scratching loudly with a finger-nail; it came from under the knapsack which served me for a pillow, and it was thrice repeated before I had time to sit up and turn about. Nothing was to be seen, nothing more was to be heard, but a few of these mysterious rustlings far and near, and the ceaseless accompaniment of the river and the frogs. I learned next day that the chestnut gardens are infected by rats; rustling, chirping, and scraping were probably all due to these; but the puzzle, for the moment, was insoluble, and I had to compose myself for sleep, as best I could, in wondering uncertainty about my neighbours.

I was wakened in the grey of the morning (Monday, 30th September) by the sound of footsteps not far off upon the stones, and opening my eyes, I beheld a peasant going by among the chestnuts by a foot-

RIVER TARN MAY 8 1982

The river at Pont de Montvert.

path that I had not hitherto observed. He turned his head neither to the right nor to the left, and disappeared in a few strides among the foliage. Here was an escape! But it was plainly more than time to be moving. The peasantry were abroad; scarce less terrible to me in my nondescript position than the soldiers of Captain Poul to an undaunted Camisard. I fed Modestine with what haste I could; but as I was returning to my sack, I saw a man and a boy come down the hillside in a direction crossing mine. They unintelligibly hailed me, and I replied with inarticulate but cheerful sounds, and hurried forward to get into my gaiters.

The pair, who seemed to be father and son, came slowly up to the plateau, and stood close beside me for some time in silence. The bed was open, and I saw with regret my revolver lying patently disclosed on the blue wool. At last, after they had looked me all over, and the silence had grown laughably embarrassing, the man demanded in

what seemed unfriendly tones:

'You have slept here?'

'Yes,' said I. 'As you see.'

'Why?' he asked.

'My faith,' I answered lightly, 'I was tired.'

He next inquired where I was going and what I had had for dinner; and then, without the least transition, '*C'est bien,*' he added, 'come along.' And he and his son, without another word, turned off to the next chestnut-tree but one, which they set to pruning. The thing had passed off more simply than I hoped. He was a grave, respectable man; and his unfriendly voice did not imply that he thought he was speaking to a criminal, but merely to an inferior.

I was soon on the road, nibbling a cake of chocolate and seriously occupied with a case of conscience. Was I to pay for my night's lodging? I had slept ill, the bed was full of fleas in the shape of ants, there was no water in the room, the very dawn had neglected to call me in the morning. I might have missed a train, had there been any in the neighbourhood to catch. Clearly, I was dissatisfied with my entertainment; and I decided I should not pay unless I met a beggar.

The valley looked even lovelier by morning; and soon the road descended to the level of the river. Here, in a place where many straight and prosperous chestnuts stood together, making an isle upon a swarded terrace, I made my morning toilette in the water of the Tarn. It was marvellously clear, thrillingly cool; the soap-suds disappeared as if by magic in the swift current, and the white boulders gave one a model for cleanliness. To wash in one of God's rivers in the open air seems to me a sort of cheerful solemnity or semi-pagan act of worship. To dabble among dishes in a bedroom may perhaps make clean the body; but the imagination takes no share in such a cleansing. I went on with a light and peaceful heart, and sang psalms to the spiritual ear as I advanced.

Suddenly up came an old woman, who point-blank demanded alms.

'Good,' thought I; 'here comes the waiter with the bill.'

And I paid for my night's lodging on the spot. Take it how you please, but this was the first and the last beggar that I met with during all my tour.

A step or two farther I was overtaken by an old man in a brown nightcap, clear-eyed, weather-beaten, with a faint excited smile. A little girl followed him, driving two sheep and a goat; but she kept in our wake, while the old man walked beside me and talked about the morning and the valley. It was not much past six; and for healthy people who have slept enough, that is an hour of expansion and of open and trustful talk.

'*Connaissez-vous le Seigneur?*' he said at length.

I asked him what Seigneur he meant; but he only repeated the question with more emphasis and a look in his eyes denoting hope and interest.

'Ah,' said I, pointing upwards, 'I understand you now. Yes, I know Him; He is the best of acquaintances.'

The old man said he was delighted. 'Hold,' he added, striking his bosom; 'it makes me happy here.' There were a few who knew the Lord in these valleys, he went on to tell me; not many, but a few. 'Many are called,' he quoted, 'and few chosen.'

'My father,' said I, 'it is not easy to say who know the Lord; and it is none of our business. Protestants and Catholics, and even those who worship stones, may know Him and be known by Him; for He has made all.'

I did not know I was so good a preacher.

The old man assured me he thought as I did, and repeated his expressions of pleasure at meeting me. 'We are so few,' he said. 'They call us Moravians here; but down in the Department of Gard, where there are also a good number, they are called Derbists, after an English pastor.'

I began to understand that I was figuring, in questionable taste, as a member of some sect to me unknown; but I was more pleased with the pleasure of my companion than embarrassed by my own equivocal position. Indeed, I can see no dishonesty in not avowing a difference; and especially in these high matters, where we have all a sufficient assurance that, whoever may be in the wrong, we ourselves are not completely in the right. The truth is much talked about; but this old man in a brown nightcap showed himself so simple, sweet, and friendly, that I am not unwilling to profess myself his convert. He was, as a matter of fact, a Plymouth Brother. Of what that involves in the way of doctrine I have no idea nor the time to inform myself; but I know right well that we are all embarked upon a troublesome world, the children of one Father, striving in many essential points to do and to become the same. And although it was somewhat in a mistake that he shook hands with me so often and showed himself so ready to receive my words, that was a mistake of the truth-finding sort. For charity begins blindfold; and only through a series of similar mis-apprehensions rises at length into a settled principle of love and patience, and a firm belief in all our fellow-men. If I deceived this good old man, in the like manner I would willingly go on to deceive others. And if ever at length, out of our separate and sad ways, we should all come together into one common house, I have a hope, to which I cling dearly, that my mountain Plymouth Brother will hasten to shake hands with me again.

Thus, talking like Christian and Faithful by the way, he and I came down upon a hamlet by the Tarn. It was but a humble place, called La Vernède, with less than a dozen houses, and a Protestant chapel on a knoll. Here he dwelt; and here, at the inn, I ordered my breakfast. The inn was kept by an agreeable young man, a stone-breaker on the road, and his sister, a pretty and engaging girl. The village schoolmaster dropped in to speak with the stranger. And these were all Protestants – a fact which pleased me more than I should have

Women returning from market, from the Albert Kahn collection of old photographs.

expected; and, what pleased me still more, they seemed all upright and simple people. The Plymouth Brother hung round me with a sort of yearning interest, and returned at least thrice to make sure I was enjoying my meal. His behaviour touched me deeply at the time, and even now moves me in recollection. He feared to intrude, but he would not willingly forego one moment of my society; and he seemed never weary of shaking me by the hand.

When all the rest had drifted off to their day's work, I sat for near half an hour with the young mistress of the house, who talked pleasantly over her seam of the chestnut harvest, and the beauties of the Tarn, and old family affections, broken up when young folk go from home, yet still subsisting. Hers, I am sure, was a sweet nature, with a country plainness and much delicacy underneath; and he who takes her to his heart will doubtless be a fortunate young man.

The valley below La Vernède pleased me more and more as I went forward. Now the hills approached from either hand, naked and crumbling, and walled in the river between cliffs; and now the valley widened and became green. The road led me past the old castle of Miral on a steep; past a battlemented monastery, long since broken up and turned into a church and parsonage; and past a cluster of black roofs, the village of Cocurès, sitting among vineyards, and meadows, and orchards thick with red apples, and where, along the highway, they were knocking down walnuts from the roadside trees, and gathering them in sacks and baskets. The hills, however much the vale might open, were still tall and bare, with cliffy battlements and here and there a pointed summit; and the Tarn still rattled through the stones with a mountain noise. I had been led, by bagmen of a picturesque turn of mind, to expect a horrific country after the heart of Byron; but to my Scottish eyes it seemed smiling and plentiful, as the weather still gave an impression of high summer to my Scottish body; although the chestnuts were already picked out by the autumn, and the poplars, that here began to mingle with them, had turned into pale gold against the approach of winter.

There was something in this landscape, smiling although wild, that explained to me the spirit of the Southern Covenanters. Those who took to the hills for conscience' sake in Scotland had all gloomy and bedevilled thoughts; for once that they received God's comfort they would be twice engaged with Satan; but the Camisards had only bright and supporting visions. They dealt much more in blood, both given and taken; yet I find no obsession of the Evil One in their records. With a light conscience, they pursued their life in these rough times and circumstances. The soul of Séguier, let us not forget, was like a garden. They knew they were on God's side, with a knowledge that has no parallel among the Scots; for the Scots, although they might be certain of the cause, could never rest confident of the person.

'We flew,' says one old Camisard, 'when we heard the sound of psalm-singing, we flew as if with wings. We felt within us an animating ardour, a transporting desire. The feeling cannot be expressed in words. It is a thing that must have been experienced to be understood. However weary we might be, we thought no more of our weariness, and grew light so soon as the psalms fell upon our ears.'

The valley of the Tarn and the people whom I met at La Vernède not only explain to me this passage, but the twenty years of suffering which those, who were so stiff and so bloody when once they betook themselves to war, endured with the meekness of children and the constancy of saints and peasants.

————————Florac————————

ON a branch of the Tarn stands Florac, the seat of a sub-prefecture, with an old castle, an alley of planes, many quaint street-corners, and a live fountain welling from the hill. It is notable, besides, for handsome women, and as one of the two capitals, Alais being the other, of the country of the Camisards.

The landlord of the inn took me, after I had eaten, to an adjoining café, where I, or rather my journey, became the topic of the afternoon. Every one had some suggestion for my guidance; and the sub-prefectorial map was fetched from the sub-prefecture itself, and much thumbed among coffee-cups and glasses of liqueur. Most of these kind advisers were Protestant, though I observed that Protestant and Catholic intermingled in a very easy manner; and it surprised me to see what a lively memory still subsisted of the religious war. Among the hills of the south-west, by Mauchline, Cumnock, or Carsphairn, in isolated farms or in the manse, serious Presbyterian people still recall the days of the great persecution, and the graves of local martyrs are still piously regarded. But in towns and among the so-called better classes, I fear that these old doings have become an idle tale. If you met a mixed company in the King's Arms at Wigton, it is not likely that the talk would run on Covenanters. Nay, at Muirkirk of Glenluce, I found the beadle's wife had not so much as heard of Prophet Peden. But these Cévenols were proud of their ancestors in quite another sense; the war was their chosen topic; its exploits were their own patent of nobility; and where a man or a race has had but one adventure, and that heroic, we must expect and pardon some prolixity of reference. They told me the country was still full of legends hitherto uncollected; I heard from them about Cavalier's descendants – not direct descendants, be it understood, but only cousins or nephews – who were still prosperous people in the scene of the boy-general's exploits; and one farmer had seen the bones of old combatants dug up into the air of an afternoon in the nineteenth century, in a field where the ancestors had fought, and the great-grandchildren were peaceably ditching.

Later in the day one of the Protestant pastors was so good as to visit me: a young man, intelligent and polite, with whom I passed an hour or two in talk. Florac, he told me, is part Protestant, part Catholic;

A village with hills beyond by René Vallette.

and the difference in religion is usually doubled by a difference in politics. You may judge of my surprise, coming as I did from such a babbling purgatorial Poland of a place as Monastier, when I learned that the population lived together on very quiet terms; and there was even an exchange of hospitalities between households thus doubly separated. Black Camisard and White Camisard, militiaman and Miquelet and dragoon, Protestant prophet and Catholic cadet of the White Cross, they had all been sabring and shooting, burning, pillaging, and murdering, their hearts hot with indignant passion; and here, after a hundred and seventy years, Protestant is still Protestant, Catholic still Catholic, in mutual toleration and mild amity of life. But the race of man, like that indomitable nature whence it sprang, has medicating virtues of its own; the years and seasons bring various harvests; the sun returns after the rain; and mankind outlives secular animosities, as a single man awakens from the passions of a day. We judge our ancestors from a more divine position; and the dust being a little laid with several centuries, we can see both sides adorned with human virtues and fighting with a show of right.

I have never thought it easy to be just, and find it daily even harder than I thought. I own I met these Protestants with a delight and a sense of coming home. I was accustomed to speak their language, in another and deeper sense of the word than that which distinguishes between French and English; for the true Babel is a divergence upon morals. And hence I could hold more free communication with the Protestants, and judge them more justly, than the Catholics. Father Apollinaris may pair off with my mountain Plymouth Brother as two guileless and devout old men; yet I ask myself if I had as ready a feeling for the virtues of the Trappist; or, had I been a Catholic, if I should have felt so warmly to the dissenter of La Vernède. With the first I was on terms of mere forbearance; but with the other, although only on a misunderstanding and by keeping on selected points, it was still possible to hold converse and exchange some honest thoughts. In this world of imperfection we gladly welcome even partial intimacies. And if we find but one to whom we can speak out of our heart freely, with whom we can walk in love and simplicity without dissimulation, we have no ground of quarrel with the world or God.

In the Valley of the Mimente

ON Tuesday, 1st October, we left Florac late in the afternoon, a tired donkey and tired donkey-driver. A little way up the Tarnon, a covered bridge of wood introduced us into the valley of the Mimente. Steep rocky red mountains overhung the stream; great oaks and chestnuts grew upon the slopes or in stony terraces; here and there was a red field of millet or a few apple-trees studded with red apples; and the road passed hard by two black hamlets, one with an old castle atop to please the heart of the tourist.

It was difficult here again to find a spot fit for my encampment. Even under the oaks and chestnuts the ground had not only a very rapid slope, but was heaped with loose stones; and where there was no timber the hills descended to the stream in a red precipice tufted with heather. The sun had left the highest peak in front of me, and the valley was full of the lowing sound of herdsmen's horns as they recalled the flocks into the stable, when I spied a bight of meadow some way below the roadway in an angle of the river. Thither I descended, and, tying Modestine provisionally to a tree, proceeded to investigate the neighbourhood. A grey pearly evening shadow filled the glen; objects at a little distance grew indistinct and melted bafflingly into each other; and the darkness was rising steadily like an exhalation. I approached a great oak which grew in the meadow, hard by the river's brink; when to my disgust the voices of children fell upon my ear, and I beheld a house round the angle on the other bank. I had half a mind to pack and be gone again, but the growing darkness moved me to remain. I had only to make no noise until the night was fairly come, and trust to the dawn to call me early in the morning. But it was hard to be annoyed by neighbours in such a great hotel.

A hollow underneath the oak was my bed. Before I had fed Modestine and arranged my sack, three stars were already brightly shining, and the others were beginning dimly to appear. I slipped down to the river, which looked very black among its rocks, to fill my can; and dined with a good appetite in the dark, for I scrupled to light a lantern while so near a house. The moon, which I had seen a pallid crescent all afternoon, faintly illuminated the summit of the hills, but not a ray fell into the bottom of the glen where I was lying. The oak rose before me like a pillar of darkness; and overhead the heartsome stars were set in the face of the night. No one knows the stars who has not slept, as the French happily put it, *à la belle étoile*. He may know all their names and distances and magnitudes, and yet be ignorant of what alone concerns mankind, – their serene and gladsome influence on the mind. The greater part of poetry is about the stars; and very justly, for they are themselves the most classical of poets. These same far-away worlds, sprinkled like tapers or shaken together like a diamond dust upon the sky, had looked not otherwise to Roland or Cavalier, when, in the words of the latter, they had 'no other tent but the sky, and no other bed than my mother earth.'

All night a strong wind blew up the valley, and the acorns fell pattering over me from the oak. Yet, on this first night of October, the air was as mild as May, and I slept with the fur thrown back.

I was much disturbed by the barking of a dog, an animal that I fear more than any wolf. A dog is vastly braver, and is besides supported by the sense of duty. If you kill a wolf, you meet with encouragement and praise; but if you kill a dog, the sacred rights of property and the domestic affections come clamouring round you for redress. At the end of a fagging day, the sharp cruel note of a dog's bark is in itself a keen annoyance; and to a tramp like myself, he represents the sedentary and respectable world in its most hostile form. There is something of the clergyman or the lawyer about this engaging animal; and if he were not amenable to stones, the boldest man would shrink from travelling afoot. I respect dogs much in the domestic circle; but on the highway, or sleeping afield, I both detest and fear them.

I was wakened next morning (Wednesday, October 2nd) by the same dog – for I knew his bark – making a charge down the bank, and then, seeing me sit up, retreating again with great alacrity. The stars were not yet quite extinguished. The heaven was of that enchanting mild grey-blue of the early morn. A still clear light began to fall, and the trees on the hillside were outlined sharply against the sky. The wind had veered more to the north, and no longer reached me in the glen; but as I was going on with my preparations, it drove a white cloud very swiftly over the hill-top; and looking up, I was surprised to see the cloud dyed with gold. In these high regions of the air, the sun was already shining as at noon. If only the clouds travelled high enough, we should see the same thing all night long. For it is always daylight in the fields of space.

As I began to go up the valley, a draught of wind came down it out of the seat of the sunrise, although the clouds continued to run overhead in an almost contrary direction. A few steps farther, and I saw a whole hillside gilded with the sun; and still a little beyond, between two peaks, a centre of dazzling brilliancy appeared floating in the sky, and I was once more face to face with the big bonfire that occupies the kernel of our system.

I met but one human being that forenoon, a dark military-looking wayfarer, who carried a game-bag on a baldric; but he made a remark that seems worthy of record. For when I asked him if he were Protestant or Catholic –

'Oh,' said he, 'I make no shame of my religion. I am a Catholic.'

He made no shame of it! The phrase is a piece of natural statistics; for it is the language of one in a minority. I thought with a smile of Bavile and his dragoons, and how you may ride rough-shod over a religion for a century, and leave it only the more lively for the friction. Ireland is still Catholic; the Cévennes still Protestant. It is not a basketful of law-papers, nor the hoofs and pistol-butts of a regiment of horse, that can change one tittle of a ploughman's thoughts. Outdoor rustic people have not many ideas, but such as they have are hardy plants, and thrive flourishingly in persecution. One who has grown a long while in the sweat of laborious noons, and under the stars at night, a frequenter of hills and forests, an old honest countryman, has, in the end, a sense of communion with the powers of the universe, and amicable relations towards his God. Like my mountain Plymouth Brother, he knows the Lord. His religion does not repose upon a choice of logic; it is the poetry of the man's experience, the philosophy of the history of his life. God, like a great power, like a great shining sun, has appeared to this simple fellow in the course of

The path at La Vernède.

years, and become the ground and essence of his least reflections; and you may change creeds and dogmas by authority, or proclaim a new religion with the sound of trumpets, if you will; but here is a man who has his own thoughts, and will stubbonly adhere to them in good and evil. He is a Catholic, a Protestant, or a Plymouth Brother, in the same indefeasible sense that a man is not a woman, or a woman not a man. For he could not vary from his faith, unless he could eradicate all memory of the past, and, in a strict and not a conventional meaning, change his mind.

The Heart of the Country

Women praying at a chapel.

I WAS now drawing near to Cassagnas, a cluster of black roofs upon the hillside, in this wild valley, among chestnut gardens, and looked upon in the clear air by many rocky peaks. The road along the Mimente is yet new, nor have the mountaineers recovered their surprise when the first cart arrived at Cassagnas. But although it lay thus apart from the current of men's business, this hamlet had already made a figure in the history of France. Hard by, in caverns of the mountain, was one of the five arsenals of the Camisards; where they laid up clothes and corn and arms against necessity, forged bayonets and sabres, and made themselves gunpowder with willow charcoal and saltpetre boiled in kettles. To the same caves, amid this multifarious industry, the sick and wounded were brought up to heal; and there they were visited by the two surgeons, Chàbrier and Tavan, and secretly nursed by women of the neighbourhood.

Of the five legions into which the Camisards were divided, it was the oldest and the most obscure that had its magazines by Cassagnas. This was the band of Spirit Séguier; men who had joined their voices with his in the 68th Psalm as they marched down by night on the archpriest of the Cévennes. Séguier, promoted to heaven, was succeeded by Salomon Couderc, whom Cavalier treats in his memoirs as chaplain-general to the whole army of the Camisards. He was a prophet; a great reader of the heart, who admitted people to the sacrament or refused them, by 'intentively viewing every man' between the eyes; and had the most of the Scriptures off by rote. And this was surely happy; since in a surprise in August, 1703, he lost his mule, his portfolios, and his Bible. It is only strange that they were not surprised more often and more effectually; for this legion of Cassagnas was truly patriarchal in its theory of war, and camped without sentries, leaving that duty to the angels of the God for whom they fought. This is a token, not only of their faith, but of the trackless country where they harboured. M. de Caladon, taking a stroll one fine day, walked without warning into their midst, as he might have walked into 'a flock of sheep in a plain,' and found some asleep and some awake and psalm-singing. A traitor had need of no recommendation to insinuate himself among their ranks, beyond 'his faculty of singing psalms'; and even the prophet Salomon 'took him into a particular friendship.' Thus, among their intricate hills, the rustic troop subsisted; and history can attribute few exploits to them but sacraments and ecstasies.

People of this tough and simple stock will not, as I have just been saying, prove variable in religion; nor will they get nearer to apostasy than a mere external conformity like that of Naaman in the house of Rimmon. When Louis XVI., in the words of the edict, 'convinced by the uselessness of a century of persecutions, and rather from necessity than sympathy,' granted at last a royal grace of toleration, Cassagnas was still Protestant; and to a man, it is so to this day. There is, indeed, one family that is not Protestant, but neither is it Catholic. It is that of a Catholic *curé* in revolt, who has taken to his bosom a schoolmistress. And his conduct, it is worth noting, is disapproved by the Protestant villagers.

'It is a bad idea for a man,' said one, 'to go back from his engagements.'

The villagers whom I saw seemed intelligent after a countrified fashion, and were all plain and dignified in manner. As a Protestant myself, I was well looked upon, and my acquaintance with history gained me further respect. For we had something not unlike a religious controversy at table, a gendarme and a merchant with whom I dined being both strangers to the place, and Catholics. The young men of the house stood round and supported me; and the whole discussion was tolerantly conducted, and surprised a man brought up among the infinitesimal and contentious differences of Scotland. The merchant, indeed, grew a little warm, and was far less pleased than some others with my historical acquirements. But the gendarme was mighty easy over it all.

It's a bad idea for a man to change,' said he; and the remark was generally applauded.

That was not the opinion of the priest and soldier at Our Lady of the Snows. But this is a different race; and perhaps the same great-heartedness that upheld them to resist, now enables them to differ in a kind spirit. For courage respects courage; but where a faith has been trodden out, we may look for a mean and narrow population. The true work of Bruce and Wallace was the union of the nations; not that they should stand apart a while longer, skirmishing upon their borders; but that, when the time came, they might unite with self-respect.

The merchant was much interested in my journey, and thought it dangerous to sleep afield.

'There are the wolves,' said he; 'and then it is known you are an Englishman. The English have always long purses, and it might very well enter into some one's head to deal you an ill blow some night.'

I told him I was not much afraid of such accidents; and at any rate judged it unwise to dwell upon alarms or consider small perils in the arrangement of life. Life itself, I submitted, was a far too risky

business as a whole to make each additional particular of danger worth regard. 'Something,' said I, 'might burst in your inside any day of the week, and there would be an end of you, if you were locked into your room with three turns of the key.'

'*Cependant*,' said he, '*coucher dehors!*'

'God,' said I, 'is everywhere.'

'*Cependant, coucher dehors!*' he repeated, and his voice was eloquent of terror.

He was the only person, in all my voyage, who saw anything hardy in so simple a proceeding; although many considered it superfluous. Only one, on the other hand, professed much delight in the idea; and that was my Plymouth Brother, who cried out, when I told him I sometimes preferred sleeping under the stars to a close and noisy alehouse, 'Now I see that you know the Lord!'

The merchant asked me for one of my cards as I was leaving, for he said I should be something to talk of in the future, and desired me to make a note of his request and reason; a desire with which I have thus complied.

A little after two I struck across the Mimente, and took a rugged path southward up a hillside covered with loose stones and tufts of heather. At the top, as is the habit of the country, the path disappeared; and I left my she-ass munching heather, and went forward alone to seek a road.

I was now on the separation of two vast watersheds; behind me all the streams were bound for the Garonne and the Western Ocean; before me was the basin of the Rhone. Hence, as from the Lozère, you can see in clear weather the shining of the Gulf of Lyons; and perhaps from here the soldiers of Salomon may have watched for the topsails of Sir Cloudesley Shovel, and the long-promised aid from England. You may take this ridge as lying in the heart of the country of the Camisards; four of the five legions camped all round it and almost within view – Salomon and Joani to the north, Castanet and Roland to the south; and when Julien had finished his famous work, the devastation of the High Cévennes, which lasted all through October and November, 1703, and during which four hundred and sixty villages and hamlets were, with fire and pickaxe, utterly subverted, a man standing on this eminence would have looked forth upon a silent, smokeless, and dispeopled land. Time and man's activity have now repaired these ruins; Cassagnas is once more roofed and sending up domestic smoke; and in the chestnut gardens, in low and leafy corners, many a prosperous farmer returns, when the day's work is done, to his children and bright hearth. And still it was perhaps the wildest view of all my journey. Peak upon peak, chain upon chain of hills ran surging southward, channelled and sculptured by the winter streams, feathered from head to foot with chestnuts, and here and there breaking out into a coronal of cliffs. The sun, which was still far from setting, sent a drift of misty gold across the hill-tops, but the valleys were already plunged in a profound and quiet shadow.

A very old shepherd, hobbling on a pair of sticks, and wearing a black cap of liberty, as if in honour of his nearness to the grave, directed me to the road for St. Germain de Calberte. There was something solemn in the isolation of this infirm and ancient creature. Where he dwelt, how he got upon this high ridge, or how he proposed to get down again, were more than I could fancy. Not far off upon my right was the famous Plan de Font Morte, where Poul with his Armenian sabre slashed down the Camisards of Séguier. This, me-thought, might be some Rip Van Winkle of the war, who had lost his comrades, fleeing before Poul, and wandered ever since upon the mountains. It might be news to him that Cavalier had surrendered, or Roland had fallen fighting with his back against an olive. And while I was thus working on my fancy, I heard him hailing in broken tones, and saw him waving me to come back with one of his two sticks. I had already got some way past him; but, leaving Modestine once more, retraced my steps.

Alas, it was a very commonplace affair. The old gentleman had forgot to ask the pedlar what he sold, and wished to remedy this neglect.

I told him sternly, 'Nothing.'

'Nothing?' cried he.

I repeated 'Nothing,' and made off.

It's odd to think of, but perhaps I thus became as inexplicable to the old man as he had been to me.

The road lay under chestnuts, and though I saw a hamlet or two below me in the vale, and many lone houses of the chestnut farmers, it was a very solitary march all afternoon; and the evening began early underneath the trees. But I heard the voice of a woman singing some sad, old, endless ballad not far off. It seemed to be about love and a *bel amoureux*, her handsome sweetheart; and I wished I could have taken up the strain and answered her, as I went on upon my invisible woodland way, weaving, like Pippa in the poem, my own thoughts with hers. What could I have told her? Little enough; and yet all the heart requires. How the world gives and takes away, and brings sweethearts near only to separate them again into distant and strange lands; but to love is the great amulet which makes the world a garden; and 'hope, which comes to all,' outwears the accidents of life, and reaches with tremulous hand beyond the grave and death. Easy to say: yea, but also, by God's mercy, both easy and grateful to believe!

We struck at last into a wide white high road carpeted with noise-less dust. The night had come; the moon had been shining for a long while upon the opposite mountain; when on turning a corner my donkey and I issued ourselves into her light. I had emptied out my brandy at Florac, for I could bear the stuff no longer, and replaced it with some generous and scented Volnay; and now I drank to the moon's sacred majesty upon the road. It was but a couple of mouth-fuls; yet I became thenceforth unconscious of my limbs, and my blood flowed with luxury. Even Modestine was inspired by this

Florac.

purified nocturnal sunshine, and bestirred her little hoofs as to a livelier measure. The road wound and descended swiftly among masses of chestnuts. Hot dust rose from our feet and flowed away. Our two shadows – mine deformed with the knapsack, hers comically bestridden by the pack – now lay before us clearly outlined on the road, and now, as we turned a corner, went off into the ghostly distance, and sailed along the mountain like clouds. From time to time a warm wind rustled down the valley, and set all the chestnuts dangling their bunches of foliage and fruit; the ear was filled with whispering music, and the shadows danced in tune. And next moment the breeze had gone by, and in all the valley nothing moved except our travelling feet. On the opposite slope, the monstrous ribs and gullies of the mountain were faintly designed in the moonshine; and high overhead, in some lone house, there burned one lighted window, one square spark of red in the huge field of sad nocturnal colouring.

At a certain point, as I went downward, turning many acute angles, the moon disappeared behind the hill; and I pursued my way in great darkness, until another turning shot me without preparation into St. Germain de Calberte. The place was asleep and silent, and buried in opaque night. Only from a single open door, some lamplight escaped upon the road to show me that I was come among men's habitations. The two last gossips of the evening, still talking by a garden wall, directed me to the inn. The landlady was getting her chicks to bed; the fire was already out, and had, not without grumbling, to be rekindled; half an hour later, and I must have gone supperless to roost.

The Last Day

WHEN I awoke (Thursday, 3rd October), and, hearing a great flourishing of cocks and chuckling of contented hens, betook me to the window of the clean and comfortable room where I had slept the night, I looked forth on a sunshiny morning in a deep vale of chestnut gardens. It was still early, and the cockcrows, and the slanting lights, and the long shadows encouraged me to be out and look round me.

St. Germain de Calberte is a great parish nine leagues round about. At the period of the wars, and immediately before the devastation, it was inhabited by two hundred and seventy-five families, of which only nine were Catholic; and it took the *curé* seventeen September days to go from house to house on horseback for a census. But the place itself, though capital of a canton, is scarce larger than a hamlet. It lies terraced across a steep slope in the midst of mighty chestnuts. The Protestant chapel stands below upon a shoulder; in the midst of the town is the quaint old Catholic church.

It was here that poor Du Chayla, the Christian martyr, kept his library and held a court of missionaries; here he had built his tomb, thinking to lie among a grateful population whom he had redeemed

from error; and hither on the morrow of his death they brought the body, pierced with two-and-fifty wounds, to be interred. Clad in his priestly robes, he was laid out in state in the church. The *curé*, taking his text from Second Samuel, twentieth chapter and twelfth verse, 'And Amasa wallowed in his blood in the highway,' preached a rousing sermon, and exhorted his brethren to die each at his post, like their unhappy and illustrious superior. In the midst of this eloquence there came a breeze that Spirit Séguier was at hand; and behold! all the assembly took to their horses' heels, some east, some west, and the *curé* himself as far as Alais.

Strange was the position of this little Catholic metropolis, a thimbleful of Rome, in such a wild and contrary neighbourhood. On the one hand, the legion of Salomon overlooked it from Cassagnas; on the other it was cut off from assistance by the legion of Roland at Mialet. The *curé* Louvrelenil, although he took a panic at the arch-priest's funeral, and so hurriedly decamped to Alais, stood well by his isolated pulpit, and thence uttered fulminations against the crimes of the Protestants. Salomon besieged the village for an hour and a half, but was beaten back. The militiamen, on guard before the *curé's* door, could be heard, in the black hours, singing Protestant psalms and holding friendly talk with the insurgents. And in the morning, although not a shot had been fired, there would not be a round of powder in their flasks. Where was it gone? All handed over to the Camisards for a consideration. Untrusty guardians for an isolated priest!

That these continual stirs were once busy in St. Germain de Calberte, the imagination with difficulty receives; all is now so quiet, the pulse of human life now beats so low and still in this hamlet of the mountains. Boys followed me a great way off, like a timid sort of lion-hunters; and people turned round to have a second look, or came out of their houses, as I went by. My passage was the first event, you would have fancied, since the Camisards. There was nothing rude or forward in this observation; it was but a pleased and wondering scrutiny, like that of oxen or the human infant; yet it wearied my spirits, and soon drove me from the street.

I took refuge on the terraces, which are here greenly carpeted with sward, and tried to imitate with a pencil the inimitable attitudes of the chestnuts as they bear up their canopy of leaves. Ever and again a little wind went by, and the nuts dropped all around me, with a light and dull sound, upon the sward. The noise was as of a thin fall of great hailstones; but there went with it a cheerful human sentiment of an approaching harvest and farmers rejoicing in their gains. Look-ing up, I could see the brown nut peering through the husk, which was already gaping; and between the stems the eye embraced an amphitheatre of hill, sunlit and green with leaves.

I have not often enjoyed a place more deeply. I moved in an atmosphere of pleasure, and felt light and quiet and content. But perhaps it was not the place alone that so disposed my spirit. Perhaps some one was thinking of me in another country; or perhaps some thought of my own had come and gone unnoticed, and yet done me good. For some thoughts, which sure would be the most beautiful, vanish before we can rightly scan their features; as though a god, travelling by our green highways, should but ope the door, give one smiling look into the house, and go again for ever. Was it Apollo, or Mercury, or Love with folded wings? Who shall say? But we go the lighter about our business, and feel peace and pleasure in our hearts.

I dined with a pair of Catholics. They agreed in the condemnation of a young man, a Catholic, who had married a Protestant girl and gone over to the religion of his wife. A Protestant born they could understand and respect; indeed, they seemed to be of the mind of an old Catholic woman, who told me that same day there was no difference between the two sects, save that 'wrong was more wrong for the Catholic,' who had more light and guidance; but this of a man's desertion filled them with contempt.

'It is a bad idea for a man to change,' said one.

It may have been accidental, but you see how this phrase pursued me; and for myself, I believe it is the current philosophy in these parts. I have some difficulty in imagining a better. It's not only a great flight of confidence for a man to change his creed and go out of his family for heaven's sake; but the odds are – nay, and the hope is – that, with all this great transition in the eyes of man, he has not changed himself a hairbreadth to the eyes of God. Honour to those who do so, for the wrench is sore. But it argues something narrow, whether of strength or weakness, whether of the prophet or the fool, in those who can take a sufficient interest in such infinitesimal and human operations, or who can quit a friendship for a doubtful process of the mind. And I think I should not leave my old creed for another, changing only words for other words; but by some brave reading, embrace it in spirit and truth, and find wrong as wrong for me as for the best of other communions.

The phylloxera was in the neighbourhood; and instead of wine we drank at dinner a more economical juice of the grape – La Parisienne, they call it. It is made by putting the fruit whole into a cask with water; one by one the berries ferment and burst; what is drunk during the day is supplied at night in water: so, with ever another pitcher from the well, and ever another grape exploding and giving out its strength, one cask of Parisienne may last a family till spring. It is, as the reader will anticipate, a feeble beverage, but very pleasant to the taste.

What with dinner and coffee, it was long past three before I left St. Germain de Calberte. I went down beside the Gardon of Mialet, a great glaring watercourse devoid of water, and through St. Etienne de Vallée Française, or Val Francesque, as they used to call it; and towards evening began to ascend the hill of St. Pierre. It was a long and steep ascent. Behind me an empty carriage returning to St. Jean du Gard kept hard upon my tracks, and near the summit overtook

Women at the well.

me. The driver, like the rest of the world, was sure I was a pedlar; but, unlike others, he was sure of what I had to sell. He had noticed the blue wool which hung out of my pack at either end; and from this he had decided, beyond my power to alter his decision, that I dealt in blue-wool collars, such as decorate the neck of the French draught-horse.

I had hurried to the topmost powers of Modestine, for I dearly desired to see the view upon the other side before the day had faded. But it was night when I reached the summit; the moon was riding high and clear; and only a few grey streaks of twilight lingered in the west. A yawning valley, gulfed in blackness, lay like a hole in created nature at my feet; but the outline of the hills was sharp against the sky. There was Mount Aigoal, the stronghold of Castanet. And Castanet, not only as an active undertaking leader, deserves some mention among Camisards; for there is a spray of rose among his laurel; and he showed how, even in a public tragedy, love will have its way. In the high tide of war he married, in his mountain citadel, a young and pretty lass called Mariette. There were great rejoicings; and the bridegroom released five-and-twenty prisoners in honour of the glad event. Seven months afterwards, Mariette, the Princess of the Cévennes, as they called her in derision, fell into the hands of the authorities, where it was like to have gone hard with her. But Castanet was a man of execution, and loved his wife. He fell on Valleraugue, and got a lady there for a hostage; and for the first and last time in that war there was an exchange of prisoners. Their daughter, pledge of some starry night upon Mount Aigoal, has left descendants to this day.

Modestine and I – it was our last meal together – had a snack upon the top of St. Pierre, I on a heap of stones, she standing by me in the moonlight and decorously eating bread out of my hand. The poor brute would eat more heartily in this manner; for she had a sort of affection for me, which I was soon to betray.

It was a long descent upon St. Jean du Gard, and we met no one but a carter, visible afar off by the glint of the moon on his extinguished lantern.

Before ten o'clock we had got in and were at supper; fifteen miles and a stiff hill in little beyond six hours!

——*Farewell, Modestine!*——

On examination, on the morning of October 3rd, Modestine was pronounced unfit for travel. She would need at least two days' repose, according to the ostler; but I was now eager to reach Alais for my letters; and, being in a civilised country of stage-coaches, I determined to sell my lady friend and be off by the diligence that afternoon. Our yesterday's march, with the testimony of the driver who had pursued us up the long hill of St. Pierre, spread a favourable notion of my donkey's capabilities. Intending purchasers were aware of an unrivalled opportunity. Before ten I had an offer of twenty-five francs; and before noon, after a desperate engagement, I sold her, saddle and all, for five-and-thirty. The pecuniary gain is not obvious, but I had bought freedom into the bargain.

St. Jean du Gard is a large place, and largely Protestant. The maire, a Protestant, asked me to help him in a small matter which is itself characteristic of the country. The young women of the Cévennes profit by the common religion and the difference of the language to go largely as governesses into England; and here was one, a native of Mialet, struggling with English circulars from two different agencies in London. I gave what help I could; and volunteered some advice, which struck me as being excellent.

One thing more I note. The phylloxera has ravaged the vineyards in this neighbourhood; and in the early morning, under some chestnuts by the river, I found a party of men working with a cider-press. I could not at first make out what they were after, and asked one fellow to explain.

'Making cider,' he said. '*Oui, c'est comme ça. Comme dans le nord!*'

There was a ring of sarcasm in his voice: the country was going to the devil.

It was not until I was fairly seated by the driver, and rattling through a rocky valley with dwarf olives, that I became aware of my bereavement. I had lost Modestine. Up to that moment I had thought I hated her; but now she was gone,

> 'And oh!
> The difference to me!'

For twelve days we had been fast companions; we had travelled upwards of a hundred and twenty miles, crossed several respectable ridges, and jogged along with our six legs by many a rocky and many a boggy by-road. After the first day, although sometimes I was hurt and distant in manner, I still kept my patience; and as for her, poor soul! she had come to regard me as a god. She loved to eat out of my hand. She was patient, elegant in form, the colour of an ideal mouse, and inimitably small. Her faults were those of her race and sex; her virtues were her own. Farewell, and if for ever –

Father Adam wept when he sold her to me; after I had sold her in my turn, I was tempted to follow his example; and being alone with a stage-driver and four or five agreeable young men, I did not hesitate to yield to my emotion.